FRASER ISLAND / SANDS OF TIME

FRASER ISLAND SANDS OF TIME

By FELICITY BAVERSTOCK / Featuring photographs by DENSEY CLYNE

From the Chris Wilcox film shown on ABC TV

CONTENTS

INTRODUCTION

INTRODUCTION

Sand, grain upon grain, accumulating over countless thousands of years has created Fraser Island, the largest island in the world composed entirely of sand. It is one of the five barrier islands lying off the east coast of Australia and is part of the greatest coastal sand deposit in the world, a shield to the continent stretching along 350 kilometres.

Fraser Island is 120 kilometres long and from five to twenty-five kilometres wide. It is 160 kilometres north of Brisbane and lies between the latitudes of 24 degrees 60 minutes and 25 degrees 50 minutes south and it is 1598 square kilometres in area, about two-thirds the size of the Australian Capital Territory. There are other huge sand deposits in the world – off the coast of Brazil, Guiana, Surinam, South Africa and Holland – but none as vast or as high as Australia's.

Fraser Island's sand hills rise to a height of 240 metres above sea level and sustain huge forests, more than forty freshwater lakes and streams flowing crystal clear over sand. The sands support a fascinating diversity of plant and animal life. The island is rich in history and its legends extend back to the time of the Aboriginal Dreaming.

Fraser Island is slowly giving up the secrets of its sands. In the 1970s it felt the glare of the national spotlight when arguments raged over whether sand mining should continue there. The scientists came to probe questions of how the island grew and how, over the millennia, time wrought changes enabling the sands to support a multitude of plant and animal life. They found forms unique to the island's sands and life forms which have adapted to the environment. Fraser Island is a series of fairly simple systems which can be studied easily and it has been the subject of investigation by experts in many scientific disciplines. Their discoveries have unravelled some of the island's mysteries and opened the doors to more questions. Its natural history is one of the great wonders of the earth and it is the subject of *Sands of Time*.

Previous page: Sand cemented by time into bands of brilliant colour.

This book came about because of the documentary film of the same name made by Chris Wilcox. The research team questioned scientists about their discoveries, talked to some of the residents and some of the visitors who seek out the island's attractions, and moved off the beaten track to the island's hinterland of high dunes and lakeland. Each member of the team fell under the spell of the great sand island and experienced some of its mystery.

All those approached for information gave their time enthusiastically, revealing aspects of Fraser Island that inspired this book, in the hope that more people may learn about the greatest sand island.

The film is a combination of the vision, talents and skills of different members of the film team; and the book, too, reflects the perceptions and reactions of three of the crew — researcher and writer, Felicity Baverstock, photographer and natural history writer, Densey Clyne, and film producer and director, Chris Wilcox. They dedicate this book to you, the reader, with the aim that some of the magic of Fraser Island will rub off as its story unfolds.

THE LARGEST
SAND ISLAND

THE LARGEST SAND ISLAND

Fraser Island, the world's largest island composed entirely of sand, lies like a great sleeping lizard basking in the sunny waters off Queensland's south east coast. The lizard's tail hugs the shoreline, its long, arched body curves outwards to the South Pacific Ocean and its head juts north into the wide scoop of Hervey Bay. Its backbone is a ridge of high sand dunes, some of the highest in the world.

Like the ancient reptiles that once stalked the earth, Fraser Island's evolution began in the misty distance of pre-history and it is only in the past few years that some of its secrets have emerged. They reveal that the island's sands, accumulating grain by grain during thousands of years, are still on the move and the sands are forever changing. Wind and weather sculptured the sands and moulded a landscape of astonishing diversity – a Utopia of golden shores, majestic mountain ranges of thick rainforests, freshwater lakes and streams of crystal clear waters.

To the Aborigines the island was K'gari, paradise, and their legend tells how the island was created.

The beautiful spirit K'gari helped the great god's messenger, Yendingie, to make the sea and the land for the people. Together they made the sea shores, the mountain ranges, the lakes and rivers. They worked so hard that K'gari became tired and lay down to rest on some rocks in the sea. When she awoke she looked around and said to Yendingie, 'I think this is the most wonderful place we have made' and pleaded with him to be allowed to stay. Finally Yendingie relented and changed her from a spirit into a beautiful island and, so she would not be lonely, he made trees and creeks which were specially mirrored so that she could look into the sky and see what Yendingie was doing. The laughing waters of the streams became her voice. He made birds and animals as well as people to keep her company.

Captain Cook recorded his voyage past the island in 1770 and thirty-

Previous page: Sand on the move – the massive force of a sandblow engulfs everything in its path as it moves inland.

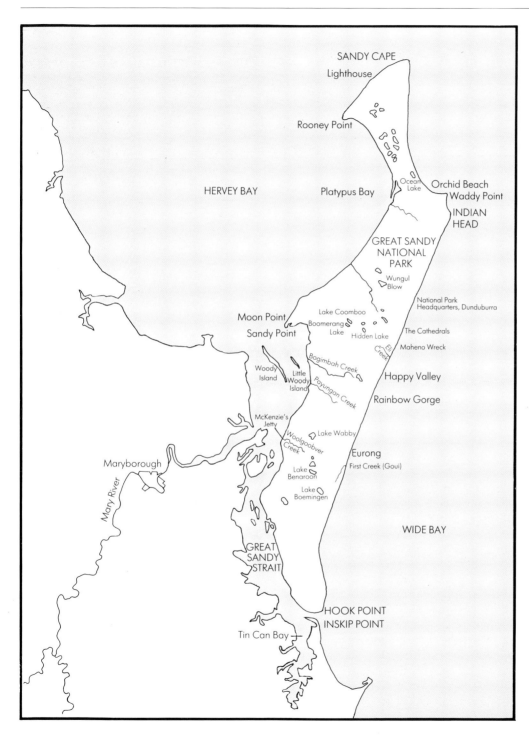

SANDY CAPE
Lighthouse

Rooney Point

HERVEY BAY   Platypus Bay   Ocean   Orchid Beach
                                          Lake   Waddy Point

                                                   INDIAN
                                                   HEAD

                          GREAT SANDY
                          NATIONAL
                          PARK

                              Wungul
                              Blow

                                                   National Park
                         Lake Coomboo   Headquarters, Dunduburra
Moon Point
               Boomerang   The Cathedrals
Sandy Point   Lake
                    Hidden Lake   Maheno Wreck
                                          Eli
                         Bogimbah Creek   Creek
Woody   Little
Island   Woody   Happy Valley
           Island   Poyungan Creek
                                                   Rainbow Gorge
McKenzie's
  Jetty
               Woolgoobver   Lake Wabby
                 Creek
                                                   Eurong
Maryborough   Lake   First Creek (Goui)
                       Benaroon
                           Lake
                         Boemingen
                                                   WIDE BAY
          GREAT
          SANDY
          STRAIT

Mary River   HOOK POINT
                                          INSKIP POINT

                 Tin Can Bay

TROPIC OF
CAPRICORN
                                          Bundaberg
                                          Maryborough

                                          Brisbane

                                          Sydney

*Fraser Island, the world's
largest sand island, hugs
the Queensland coast just
south of the Tropic of
Capricorn. It is part of the
Great Sandy Region, the
world's greatest coastal
sand deposit.*

two years later Matthew Flinders explored part of its shores. Shipwrecks around its coastline bear witness to its treacherous shoals. The most notorious wreck was that of the *Stirling Castle* in 1836. The dramatic ordeal of her captain, James Fraser, and the story of the rescue of his wife, Eliza, have been the stuff of heroic tales since.

For more than a century white settlers harvested the natural treasures of Fraser Island. Timber and minerals were taken, cattle runs and farms established and a horse stud on the island supplied stock for the Indian Army. The brumbies which

Opposite: A stream of crystal clear water flows over a pure white sandy bed as it winds through the rainforest.

Below: Dappled light flickers through the leafy canopy of the rainforest.

Left: Tall and straight, the trees of the rainforest reach up to the sun. The forest giants first attracted timber harvesters more than 120 years ago.

now run wild on the island are the descendants of those animals. Fraser Island's history is coloured by stories of its early European settlers and, more recently, by stirring events connected with efforts to stop the mining of its sands. Today the mining and farming have ceased but Fraser Island still draws visitors to its breathtaking natural wonders.

The secret of Fraser Island is sand. All life on the island, the abundant profusion of plants and animals, depends on the sand to grow and thrive. Some species have adapted to survive in the sand – which most people regard as lifeless, barren, infertile – in intriguing ways. The discovery of creatures and plants new to the realms of natural history has led to the questioning of long-held views and opinions about other parts of the world and opened up avenues of research in other countries. In 1976 an insect, a member of the grasshopper family new to science, was discovered on the island and named the Cooloola Monster after the south east Queensland region where other specimens have been located. The island provides a vast laboratory for scientific investigation and gradually the great sand mass is relinquishing some of its age-old mysteries.

Scientists and holidaymakers alike marvel at the island's variety of plants, which range from grasses struggling to maintain a hold in the windblown sands of the ocean beach to huge woodland giants like the *satinay,* the turpentine tree unique to Fraser Island with valuable termite-resistant qualities, to a wealth of heathland wildflowers and, on the west coast, clumps of mangroves growing among the fossilised remains of ancient forests. The island's rainforest pockets are among the world's wonders; they are some of the highest growing on sand in the world and sustain the 'living fossil', the *Angiopteris* fern, a remnant of the steamy life of earth 250 million years ago. Only a few of these splendid plants are known to exist and some are on Fraser Island.

More than 300 species of bird have been recorded on Fraser Island – more than in Great Britain – and it provides sanctuary for world-wandering migratory birds such as sandpipers, dotterels and godwits after their 13 000 kilometre flight from Siberia before dispersing south. The birds again assemble on the island's northern tip before the return journey to their nesting grounds beyond the Bering Sea. Colourful kingfishers, parrots, honeyeaters, pigeons, robins, flycatchers and magnificent birds of prey make their homes on the island.

A modern-day phenomenon of the island is the annual 'tailor run' when, for three months of the year during August, September and October, the ocean beaches are transformed as fishermen come in their thousands to catch the tailor fish which come from as far south as Victoria to spawn in the warm sea currents off the island. Fraser Island is the most northerly point where the tailor appear and why this is so is a puzzle yet to be unravelled.

Fishermen come in four-wheel-drive vehicles bringing elaborate equipment and gear to set up their camps on the foredunes, turning the tranquil stretch of golden sand along the island's Seventy Mile Beach into a busy thoroughfare. Their methods are in sharp contrast to those of the Aborigines of earlier times when spears where the only tools. But Aborigines did have special assistance. They would dig with their spears in the sand at the edge of the surf and, it is said, in some mysteri-ous way, dolphins out at sea would respond to the signals and herd the fish towards the beach where the Aborigines were waiting. The dolphins were rewarded with feeds of tailor. Each Aborigine had his own dolphin – it was given a name and custodianship was handed down from father to son.

Many people who visit Fraser Island absorb something of its special qualities of isolation and remoteness; its visual beauties and patterns of nature refresh those seeking the solace of wilderness. The island has been the source of creative inspiration for writers, artists, musicians and film-makers of past and present generations, Aboriginal and European, on all of whom the place has left its imprint.

But the island's shifting sands are fragile, vulnerable to the pressures it is increasingly having to bear from the impact of many visitors. Its creatures can defend themselves against natural predators, but the island which sustains them cannot always defend itself against the uncontrolled ravages of man.

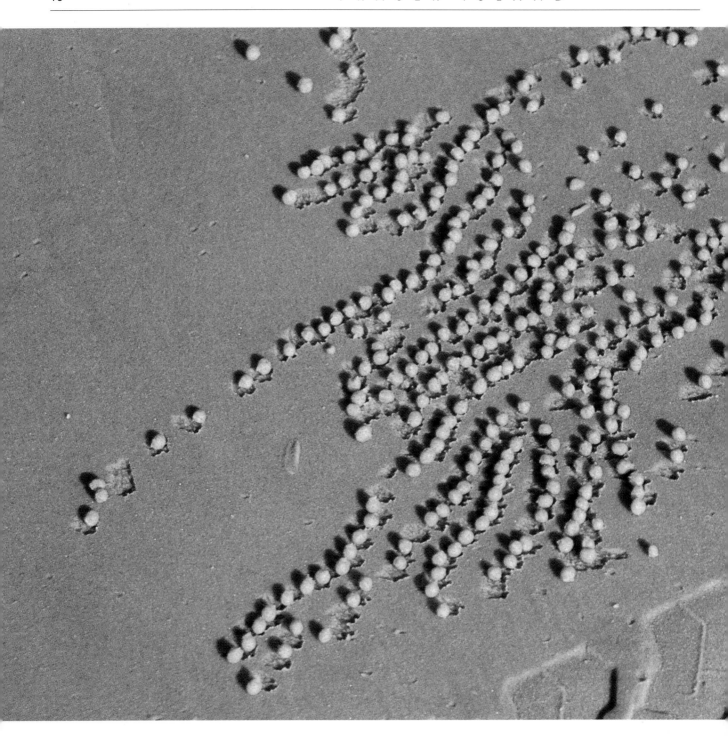

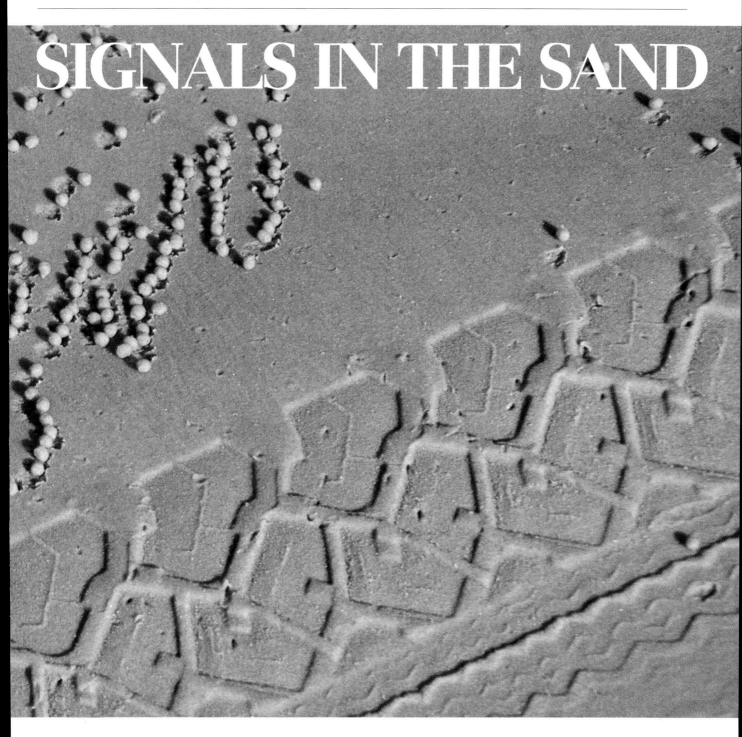

SIGNALS IN THE SAND

SIGNALS IN THE SAND

Blown by the winds, the sands of Fraser Island are always on the move. Layers of sand are episodes in the 500 000-year history of the island, revealed as the winds uncover them, buried as time moves on. Ancient middens scattered on the dunes are evidence of Aboriginal life on the island in the past; the rusting remains of old car bodies and piles of tins slowly being swallowed beneath the sands are signs of more modern man.

Previous page: Washed daily by the tides, the beach records passing life. Evidence of crabs' feeding and tyre tracks are transient imprints along the sand highway.

The Aborigines may have been part of the island for as long as 30 000 years. Carbon dating has given positive proof that Aborigines lived on the dunes from 300 AD. More than 200 midden sites on Fraser Island have been investigated. Three main groups lived there at various times of the year, a total of about 2000 people in small family clans. Each group occupied its own defined territory and was joined by other members of the tribes who came in bark canoes from the mainland for the winter fishing season. The Ngulgbara roamed the northern third of the island, the Badjala the central section and the Dulingbara occupied the south. A derivation of the Aborigines' name for the island lives on in Carree, the northernmost parish of Fraser Island.

The Aborigines were tall, well-built people, a fact noted by Matthew Flinders who landed on the northern coast during his explorations in the *Investigator* in 1802. In *Voyages in Terra Australis,* Flinders recorded his meeting with the Aborigines and the exchanges of gifts – 'hatchets and other testimonials'. He watched fishing parties casting scoop nets made of bark into the sea and observed hard, bony tumours on the wrists of the fishermen. He assumed they were caused by the stretchers of the scoops hitting the wrist each time they were thrown. The Aborigines also trapped fish in nets fixed to a bow held by several men who beat the water to frighten the fish and herd them into the net.

The Fraser Islanders painted their bodies with ochre mixed with resin, each tribe choosing different colours to distinguish its members. The men also decorated their chests with cicatrices, ornamental scars of raised flesh. A practice common to mainland Aborigines of Moreton Bay, amputation of the first joint of the right hand little finger, was observed in some of the women.

The Aborigines lived in tripod-style bark shelters, moving camp as the seasons and the food supplies dictated and on the death of a member of the group. They made the most of every available food supply. The succulent shellfish of the ocean beach, particularly the pipis, the eugaries or 'wongs' were favoured; animals were hunted; plants provided food, materials for tools and utensils and were sources of cures for ailments. Grass trees – *Xanthorrea* – served many useful purposes: their flower spikes became spear shafts; their seeds were crushed for a kind of flour; the base of the leaves was eaten raw or cooked; and the flowers, soaked in water, produced a sweet drink. The pandanus, the breadfruit tree or screw pine growing behind the beach and along the creek banks, was another valuable plant. At its peak during the dry season in September its nuts were collected, roasted and eaten, an edible substance was prepared from the trunk and the foliage was woven into baskets. The Aborigines also found a way of overcoming the poisonous properties of the fruits of the *macrozamia* – the ancient plant belonging to the primitive cycads. The bright red fruits were soaked in running water for several days before being mashed.

They recognised clues in their surroundings as guides in their hunting and gathering. The time when kangaroos were fat was when the fern leaf wattle was in bloom; when the wild passion fruit was ripe the carpet snake was ready for eating; the time for turtles was when the river chestnuts were in flower and the river mussels were at their best when the water lily put on its floral display.

The sand island had no stone for the Aborigines' implements and rock had to be brought across from the mainland. The little islet in the channel, Woody Island, was one source of raw materials for their tools and weapons. Today the sands drift back and forth across the discarded shards and remnants of the Aborigines' armament factories of the past.

The Aborigines introduced Australia's wild dog, the dingo, to the

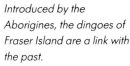

Introduced by the Aborigines, the dingoes of Fraser Island are a link with the past.

island. Isolation on the island has kept the animals free of the contamination which has affected dingoes on the mainland and today Fraser Island's dingo population of between 200 and 300 is regarded as the purest strain of dingo remaining in eastern Australia. In recent years the dingoes have suffered from contact with domestic dogs brought to the island, from distemper and parvo virus, although the island's dingoes have preyed on domestic dogs rather than interbred with them. The dingoes feed on small animals and birds; they scavenge from camps and are less distrustful of people.

The first recorded contact the island's Aborigines had with Europeans was in 1770 when Captain James Cook sailed past on his voyage of discovery along Australia's eastern coastline. But two clay pipes, of the type used in Holland in the 17th century and found in middens, suggest that Dutch mariners sailed these waters two centuries before the great English navigator. Cook named Indian Head, one of the three rocky points on the island's ocean shoreline, after seeing the native people assembled there. For 100 years the Aborigines commemorated Cook's passage in a corroboree

in which they recited a poem composed to celebrate the strange sight of the *Endeavour* as she sailed past and over the horizon:

These strangers, where are
    they going
Where are they trying to steer
They must be in that place,
    Thoorvour, it is there
See the smoke coming in
    from the sea
These men must be burying
    themselves like sandcrabs
They disappear like the smoke.

Their last glimpse of the *Endeavour* was as she cleared Breaksea Spit which they called Thoorvour. In recent years there has been a systematic attempt to restore the Aborigines' names for places on the island.

Matthew Flinders made two visits to the area, both in winter. On his first, in August 1799 in the sloop *Norfolk,* he sailed up Hervey Bay but did not realise the great sand mass was an island. The ship's course at night was directed by Aborigines' camp fires on the ocean shore. His first impression of the place was not favourable.

'Nothing can well be imagined more barren than this peninsula' he

Stalwart sentinel of the island's east coast, Indian Head was named by Captain Cook in 1770. It is one of three rocky head lands guarding the ocean shore.

wrote. Three years later he landed at Bool Creek, south west of Sandy Cape. Robert Brown, the botanist aboard the *Investigator,* collected plant specimens and named a new genus, *Jacksonia,* the dogwood, after George Jackson, a distinguished colleague. Flinders recorded the entrance to the channel at the south of the sand mass but made no attempt to enter it.

It was another twenty years before Europeans established that the great sand mass was an island. Captain William Edwardson, on a mission directed by Governor Brisbane to find a river location suited to a penal settlement, sailed up the channel between the island and the mainland. He recorded the 'island which is seventy miles in length and in some parts fourteen – fifteen miles in width'. He failed to find the river emptying into the channel opposite the island – the Mary River – and assumed that Tin Can Bay, the long, narrow inlet at the south of the island, was a river mouth. The island was named Great Sandy Island.

The district was explored by Andrew Petrie, a member of one of Queensland's great pioneering families and the former supervisor of Public Works in the infant colony of Moreton Bay. When the penal settlement closed at Moreton Bay in 1842 he sought new lands suitable for grazing by free settlers. Petrie had as his guide an escaped convict, David Bracewell, known as Wandi by the Aborigines with whom he had lived. With another escaped convict befriended by the Aborigines, James Davis, known by his native name as Durumboi, Petrie explored the Moonaboola River and named it Mary in honour of the wife of Governor Fitzroy who had met her death in a riding accident near Sydney. They found stands of kauri pine near the entrance to the river. Another convict, John Fahy, also lived with the native inhabitants at Wide Bay; he remained there for about twelve years as a fugitive.

In 1836 Great Sandy Island was the setting for an event which gained it notoriety and fame, which became the source of many legends and which gave it its name. This was the ordeal of Eliza Fraser, shipwrecked and cast on the island at the mercy of its native people.

Mrs Fraser was aboard the brig *Stirling Castle* of which her husband, Captain James Fraser, was master. The ship was in ballast, bound for Singapore from Sydney, when, on the night of May 22, 1836, she struck a reef in the Great Barrier Reef.

Eliza, her husband and the crew of about sixteen put into the ship's two boats to sail back to Moreton Bay, 1600 kilometres to the south. During the six weeks' voyage Eliza gave birth to a baby who died. The two boats parted company, one sailing south in search of rescue. The boat with Captain and Mrs Fraser, leaking and low in water supplies, landed on the beach of the island near Waddy Point on June 26.

They were confronted by hostile Aborigines whose friendly attitudes to Europeans had been destroyed by appalling acts of cruelty committed on their mainland compatriots by the settlers. Captain Fraser was fatally speared and Eliza was taken captive. She was stripped of her clothes, forced to hard manual labour and ill-treated until her rescue by an ex-convict, John Graham, who used knowledge gained from living with the Aborigines for six years to sneak into the camp of Eliza's captors.

Controversy and uncertainty surrounded Eliza's story but after it spread the island was known as Fraser Island. The amazing narrative kindled the imagination of artists and writers among whom are Sidney Nolan who, after a visit to the island in the 1940s, painted a series of pictures based on the Eliza Fraser legend, and Patrick White who used her story as the core of his novel, *A Fringe of Leaves.*

THE SANDS UNDER CHALLENGE

THE SANDS UNDER CHALLENGE

The waters of Fraser Island have claimed many ships. One of the most famous this century was the *Maheno,* once pride of her line, a veteran of World War One and holder of the record for the crossing between Auckland and Sydney in 1905, the year she was launched. One of the earliest turbine-driven passenger steamers, she first served on the coastal run between Melbourne and Sydney and across the Tasman, then, as a hospital ship, she made about forty trips between France and England in 1915 carrying thousands of wounded. Her useful days over, she left Sydney in July 1935 under tow for Japan to be scrapped.

Previous page: Relics of former forests scatter the western shore; over time, moving sand buried the trees and revealed their skeletons on the beach along Great Sandy Strait.

Off Fraser Island the towline snapped in a heavy blow. The currents and winds were too much for the *Maheno* and she drifted ashore. She has been gently rusting away on the beach ten miles north of Happy Valley for more than fifty years, slowly being swallowed by the sand. At the beginning of World War Two, she was a target for bombing practice for the air force. A picturesque wreck, she has been invaded by numerous forms of sea life: barnacles and sea anemones encrust her hull, cormorants use her salt-fretted superstructure as a vantage point.

Wrecks off the island were so frequent last century that a lighthouse was proposed and plans were drawn up. The Sandy Cape Lighthouse is a thirty metre high iron tower of tapered sections fabricated in England. They were landed at Rooney's Point and hauled by bullocks to the site. On May 19, 1870, the light was switched on and the beam was visible from thirty eight kilometres out at sea. Now operated by electricity, the lighthouse staff make meteorological observations which are stepped up in the cyclone season from the beginning of

December to the end of April. A small village grew around the lighthouse. From 1880 to 1896 Miss Shirley Lovell was the school teacher there. A keen naturalist, she made detailed notes and a collection of plants on the island. Her records made a major contribution to the island's natural history. One of the island's sundews, the carnivorous plants, *Drosera lovellae,* small, deep red and ground-dwelling, and *Pithecolobium lovellae,* the bacon wood tree which is almost confined to Fraser Island, were named after her. She also discovered another sundew, *Drosera pygmaea.*

Two discoveries in the 1860s were to have serious implications for the island's future. The first of these was in 1862 when valuable stands of timber were found. Andrew Petrie's son, Tom, and a Scottish-born timber merchant, William Pettigrew, who had started the first steam-operated sawmill in Brisbane, surveyed stands of kauri pine on the island. The first logs were milled at Maryborough in 1863 at a place called Dundathu, the Aborigines' name for kauri pine. White beech soon followed. The commercial potential of timber put an end to plans for the island to become an Aboriginal reserve.

Then, in 1867, gold was discovered at Gympie on the mainland, giving a boost to the growing port of Maryborough. Fraser Island became a staging post for supplies and the site of the quarantine and immigration station. The native inhabitants were exposed to white men's diseases and the evils of alcohol and opium. Tribal conflicts between the different groups of Aborigines were provoked by the newcomers and there were bloody battles.

Balarrgan, a mission station, was opened in October, 1870, at North White Cliffs by the Rev Edward Fuller in the hope that a farm could be run, but the sandy soil beat him and within two years it closed.

In 1897 the mission was reinstated by the Government and was transferred to Bogimbah Creek. Fifty-one Aborigines from Maryborough were rounded up to start the settlement, a pitiful remnant of the thousands who had once occupied the district, and it was placed under the control of the Protector, Archibald Meston. Although he believed that the people's traditional culture could be revived the project was doomed. As many as nineteen different language groups were thrown together at one time and the ravaging effects of European impact took their toll.

The salt-fretted hull of the Maheno, rusting away on the ocean beach, is all that remains of the once-proud liner which went aground off Fraser Island in 1935.

Within seven years ninety-eight Aborigines died of disease or malnutrition. Bogimbah was abandoned in 1905 and the remaining people were transferred to missions on the mainland. Deportation of Aborigines from Fraser Island continued until the 1930s when the last-known member of the Badjala tribe was transported to the mainland. The Fraser Island Badjala Committee was set up in the late 1970s. Its aim was to retrieve some of the heritage of tribes who lived on the island until late last century.

Timber has been harvested from Fraser Island for more than 120 years. The prized trees – kauri and hoop pine, beech, blackbutt and tallow wood among them – grew to forest giants in the sandy beds of the greatest sand island. The timber has found its way all round the world. Fraser Island's timber was used in massive constructions such as the Suez Canal and London's Tilbury Docks. Between 1919 and 1925 four sawmills were working on the island and the forests were threaded with steam tramlines for transporting the logs to the shore. Today the logs go to Maryborough by barge.

Tom Petrie's son, Walter, a forester, established the first permanent forestry operations on the island – at Bogimbah Creek in 1913. Three years later trial plantings continued experimental methods in silviculture first started in the island's sandy soils in the 1880s.

Bullocks, in teams of twenty yolked together, hauled the logs – two loads a day – through the forests for punting or to the tramlines. The timber-getting teams stayed on the island for about a month at a time, working six days a week. The early timber-getters were a rough lot, hardened by the tough life. One creek was known in the heyday of its sawmilling as Foulmouth Creek from the language that rang through the bush.

At the peak of McKenzie's sawmills in the early 1920s one hundred men – some with their families – worked and lived on Fraser Island. There was a school with an enrolment of about forty. The bullocky era and the steam trams continued until 1937 when motorised transport took over.

Between 1908 and 1925 almost the entire island came under the control of the State Forestry Department. In 1919 H. McKenzie, a Sydney timber merchant who bought the ten-year rights to timber on 4040 hectares (10 000 acres) on the island, began operating the first mill there. It was built at the old quarantine station, linked to a jetty by tramline. In the six years that followed McKenzie operated another three sawmills with tramlines weaving through the forest to loading points on the west coast. It was a thriving enterprise; then troubles struck. A serious fire was blamed on one of McKenzie's engines and industrial arguments raged. The sawmills were forced to close.

In 1926 the Forestry Department bought the tramline, wharves and installations and continued working them until the effects of the Depression hit in the 1930s. In World War Two McKenzie's camp served as a commando training unit. Members

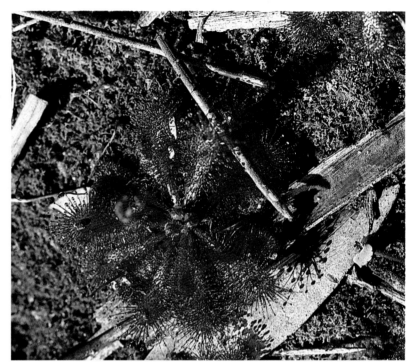

of the famous Z Force trained there. Z Force carried out the 1943 raid known as Jaywick when 40 000 tonnes of Japanese shipping were blown up in Singapore Harbour.

Today about two thirds of Fraser Island is state forest. It supplies about forty per cent of the Maryborough timber industry's raw material. The Forestry Department carries out a program of selecting trees for harvest so that the essential structure of the forest is retained and regeneration is supplemented by planting blackbutt.

Cattle were first taken to the island in the late 1860s. The Fraser

Shirley Lovell, during her term as schoolteacher last century, made a study of the island's flora. She identified several carnivorous (insect-eating) plants including this one which clings to the lake shores and around the swamps.

Island Run, a parcel of about sixty-four square kilometres of land near Eurong on the eastern side of the island, grazed about forty head of cattle and grazing continued until the late 1970s when the last stragglers were rounded up and shot.

The brumbies – the wild horses roaming Fraser Island – have a proud ancestry. There are about 200 animals, descendants of Arabs and Clydesdales brought to the island in the 1870s as the nucleus of a breeding stud. Pure-bred Arabs were supplied to the Indian Army from the Fraser Island Run. A ship with horses aboard foundered off Sandy Cape and some of the horses struggled ashore to run wild on the island where they interbred over the years with Clydesdales which had escaped into the scrub. The brumbies range over the eastern side of the island in groups of one stallion to five or six mares and choose the ocean beach foredunes as their favourite pastures when the seasons are good. The wild horses are said to destroy delicate foredune plants holding the sand together but with every mouthful they eat a few grains of sand and its abrasive effects are said to shorten their lifespan. By the time the foals reach about eighteen months of age their hooves start to spread so that

their feet land flat on the sandy ground.

The 1970s focussed national attention on Fraser Island when the fight to stop sand mining began. Until then the island was the peaceful preserve of the timber men, the few score permanent residents and a handful of visitors, mostly people from the neighbouring mainland who stayed in a cluster of holiday shacks at Happy Valley on the east coast. In the 1960s, as people began to discover the unique attractions of the island, Eurong Village developed and Orchid Beach resort followed.

In 1961 a proposal to hand over Fraser Island to the people of Nauru as compensation for the mining of superphosphate on their homeland was rejected on the grounds that the soil was too sandy for agriculture.

Minerals such as rutile, zircon, ilmenite and monazite are part of the valuable riches yielded by the black sands along Australia's east coast from Newcastle to Gladstone. Last century attempts to take coal from the sands of Fraser Island were thwarted by the sand collapsing into the pits and in the 1960s oil prospecting was carried out on the island. The storm over sand mining broke when, in January 1971, the miners applied to extend leases held on the island since the mid 1960s. Mining operations started in December, 1971.

The mining and further lease applications caused a public clamour and conservation groups raised loud angry voices. The fight was long and bitter. The Federal Government commissioned the Fraser Island Environmental Enquiry which survived several High Court challenges and finally handed down its findings in October, 1976, recommending banning of export of mineral sands from Fraser Island. Mining ceased on December 31, 1976 and that month the island became the first item listed on the Australian Register of the National Estate. The International Union for Conservation of Nature and Natural Resources, advisors to UNESCO's World Heritage Committee, included Fraser Island and its companion mainland sandmass of Cooloola in a list of 221 natural sites proposed for the World Heritage List.

In December, 1971, an area of 23 000 hectares on the island's northern end was declared a national park seventy-eight years after the Australian Association of Science had proposed the entire island be proclaimed a national park. By 1978, after two further additions, the park contained 49 000 hectares. It is called the Great Sandy National Park and is administered by the Queensland National Parks and Wildlife Service with its headquarters at Dundubara.

The Fraser Island Defenders Organisation, FIDO, rallied conservationists in 1971 under its symbol of a bulldog, a breed known for its tenacity, and still perseveres in its watchdog role. The driving force behind the organisation is John Sinclair, in 1977 pronounced the Australian of the Year by the national newspaper, *The Australian.* The battle to stop sand mining is won but FIDO continues its fight against what it sees as the harmful effects of logging and destruction of the island's natural environment by increasing urban development and uncontrolled numbers of visitors. FIDO campaigns vigorously for a proper plan of management for Fraser Island, asserting that, by 2000, the entire island should become a national park.

The Fraser Island Public Access Act 1985, to be administered by the Queensland Department of Forestry and the Queensland National Parks and Wildlife Service, is expected to come into effect in 1986 to control and manage public vehicle access.

AEONS OF TIME
Building the Great Sandcastle

AEONS OF TIME
Building the
Great Sandcastle

Fraser Island owes its existence to the most violent forces of nature. Cataclysmic storms, wild cyclones, furious winds and lashing gales set in motion the events which created the great sand island. For millions of years wind and water wearing away at the face of Australia produced the sand particles which were slowly swept by the waves up the continent's eastern coastline to be distributed gradually, grain by grain, on Queensland's south eastern shores.

Much of the island's raw material – the sand – began as sediments torn from the banks of the big, swiftly-flowing rivers which run to the sea from the Great Dividing Range, the spine of mountains along Australia's eastern side. During floods high boulders were tumbled and pulverised in the turbulent waters to join the sediment flow. As the sediments spilled into the Pacific Ocean they combined with particles of rock ground by the surf from the headlands of the shore to be swept into vast deposits on the ocean floor. This process, colossal in scale, yet imperceptible, is as old as the continent itself and it continues still.

Winds and their offspring, waves and currents, were and still are the prime movers in shaping Fraser Island. The prevailing winds of Australia's east coast are from the south east. They sweep over the southern ocean to hit the coastline, not at right angles, but to blow over it in a north westerly direction. With the currents whipped into action by the winds came the sand, to be lifted off the ocean beds, carried north and dumped on obstructions such as rocky outcrops in the sea and the bulging shape of the continent's coastline.

A quick look at the map shows Australia's resemblance to an enormous butterfly with its most easterly and westerly points the tips of the butterfly's wings. On their northward journeys along each side

Previous page: Forever at the mercy of the winds, the sands of Fraser Island are sculptured into valleys, rifts, cliffs and canyons.

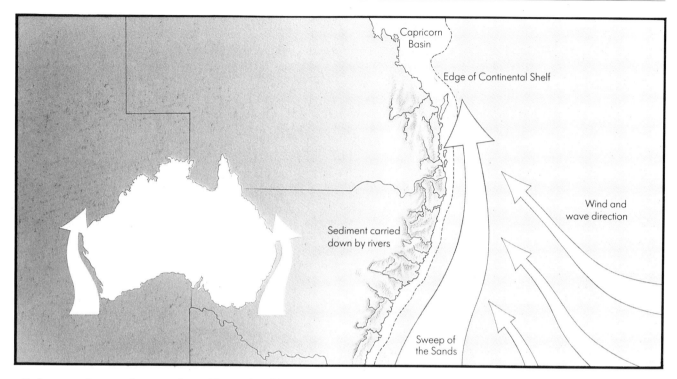

of the continent the sands collected at these points in huge deposits on the shores. Unlike other parts of the world, such as Texas, where sand has also been borne by the tides to collect on the coast, Australia's butterfly wings are lowlands offering little resistance, such as rocky headlands and steep shoreline cliffs, to the sands. For sixty million years the waves and currents have laid down their cargoes of sand to blanket the lowlands of the coast and line the continental shelf which hugs the shore.

The Great Sandy Region of south east Queensland encompasses Fraser Island and its neighbouring coastal sand dune landscape of Cooloola, the lands east of the Noosa River and the strait separating the island from the mainland. The region is 350 000 hectares in area and is part of the 1200 kilometre stretch of coastal dunes from Newcastle in New South Wales to Gladstone in Queensland and is the greatest coastal sand deposit in the world. The area contains numerous islands which have developed as sand built up behind rocks in the sea. Fraser Island, North and South Stradbroke, Moreton and Bribie Islands are called the barrier islands.

Australia's coastline is shaped like an enormous butterfly whose wingtips are the most easterly and westerly points and where the sands, borne northwards by currents, have collected along the shores.

Sand, accumulating against rocky outcrops in the sea, gradually built the largest sand island in the world. The outcrops, on the east coast, are the only true rocks on Fraser Island.

The region's north boundary is the Tropic of Capricorn (23 degrees 26 minutes south) which has given its name to the vast underwater basin lying to the north of Fraser Island. The location of the Capricorn Basin is one of the reasons for most of the huge sand masses being contained in the Great Sandy Region and not extending further north where they would engulf and alter the character of the coral islands of the Great Barrier Reef. The Capricorn Basin acts as a sink, dragging the sand over its lip to settle in its sheltered depths as the sand-bearing currents move northwards. The inshore current is

Above: The forces of nature and time have fused coloured sands along parts of the ocean shore into strange, tortured shapes. They are the Teewah Sands, mystery sands whose origins are shrouded in the past.

Left: In fiery blazes of colour, the Teewah Sands rise like fortresses above the beach.

countered by a southerly set which helps to inhibit the northward flow of sand. Once unloaded of their cargoes of sediment, the seas wash clear and reach the shores of the Great Barrier Reef islands free of the bulk of their sandy burden. Fraser Island itself is an impediment to the sands' northerly progress.

Fraser Island began to form as sand became trapped behind three rocky outcrops in the sea. Eroded and stripped bare by wind and waves these little rocky sentinels emerging from the sea on the island's ocean shoreline are Indian Head, Middle Rocks and Waddy Point and, with one other rocky outcrop on the west coast, they are the only hard rocks on the island. They are of volcanic origin, dating from the Oligocene epoch of thirty-eight million years ago.

Slowly, inexorably, over two million years, the beaches and dunes developed behind the three headlands and Fraser Island grew like a huge sandcastle, rising more than 200 metres above sea level at its highest point and extending 600 metres below it to sit firmly on the seabed. Fraser Island is 120 kilometres long and from five to twenty-five kilometres wide. Always at the mercy of the winds and weather that sculpt and mould its shores, the huge sandcastle is not likely to be washed away at the next tide.

The south east currents are also responsible for scouring the long, curving beaches of the ocean's shores. They have developed in the shape known as zeta curves, or reversed Js. Seventy Mile Beach, with its southern tip Inskip Point and its northern end Indian Head, is one of the longest beaches in the world. Another zeta curve is being scoured along the shore further north between Waddy Point and Sandy Cape.

The narrow channel dividing the island from the mainland has been prevented from filling with sand because it is constantly dredged by the outflow from the Mary River which enters the sea opposite the island at about halfway along its western coast. The river's floodwaters regularly scour the channel, helping to keep it open. Its waters are shallow and the Aborigines are said to have waded across to the island from the mainland.

Sands washed onto the coast from the sea are known as oceanic and are aeolian, or wind-blown, the term derived from the ruler of the winds in Greek mythology, King Aeolus. They are mainly grains of silica or quartz, one of the most common minerals of the earth's crust. The oceanic sands of northern New South Wales and south east Queensland contain about two per cent of other, heavy minerals which settle on the beaches and foredunes. These valuable mineral deposits were mined on Fraser Island from 1971 until 1976. The sandy shores of this part of the continent yielded the world's largest supplies of rutile, the mineral used for industrial purposes such as making pigments for paints and in the manufacture of false teeth, imparting a pale yellow colour for a natural appearance. Ilmenite, a source of titanium used in aircraft construction, zircon, a derivative of which is used in the construction of nuclear reactors, and feldspar, part of ceramic and glass making processes, are other heavy minerals found and mined in the region. The quartz grains themselves are coated with minute quantities of other minerals which provide important nutriments for the island's plants, many of which have forged strange links with the sand in order to extract the properties vital in their growth.

The great belts of oceanic sands have been laid under and over spectacular, coloured seams of sands which are exposed along the coast and which draw tourists to marvel at their blazing display of fiery reds, oranges, yellows and browns. They are the Teewah Sands and are very old, considered by some scientists to have been laid down almost 800 000 years ago. No accurate dating methods are available to give a precise age to these mystery sands. They are distinctly different from the oceanic sands. Outcrops of Teewah Sands are bared in places among the dunes.

Their brilliant colouring is thought to be the result of laterisation, a natural process occurring in tropical soils such as Queensland's where exposure to weathering and leaching causes the different mineral components, particularly iron, to decompose and percolate through the sandy layers. The Teewah Sands contain small amounts of clay which help to bind them and, where they emerge along the surf beaches of the region, the weather has carved them into cliffs and ridges of breathtaking beauty.

The Cathedrals, near Akuna Creek which enters the sea on Seventy Mile Beach, rise sheer to a height of fifteen metres, their sunset colours reflected in the wet sands as the waves wash up to their feet at high tide.

Scientists probing with their drill bores into the cliffs have suggested that the Teewah Sands may have originated on the mainland and that they were blown eastwards during long-ago periods of dryness and fierce winds. Others have surmised that they are the remains of an old coastal landscape which once extended further east than it does today. Whatever their origin the Teewah Sands are ancient and their beginning is shrouded by time. Fraser Island presents an intriguing list of unexplained questions to science: only a few of its secrets have been revealed in the last few years

Opposite: Spectacular cliffs of coloured sands are exposed along Fraser Island's ocean coast.

Above: The towers and buttresses of The Cathedrals are etched in vivid contrast against the sky.

Below: Minerals in the ancient Teewah Sands give brilliant sunset colours.

since it came under the scrutiny of researchers from many disciplines.

The drill probes uncovering the ancient fossil remains of plants in the layers of sands along the shoreline have indicated how varying sea levels existed at different times in the earth's long history. During the four major glacial periods of the Pleistocene Age (up to two million years ago) the icecaps of the poles slowly expanded and sea levels dropped, stranding sand plains of the ocean floor along the fringes of the great land masses. The ice ages were separated by periods of relatively warmer temperatures; the Great Interglacial, lasting 200 000 years, occurred between the second and third glacial epochs. The glacials were accompanied by winds of incredible velocity and strength which tore across the face of the globe whipping up the surface sediments and depositing them elsewhere. Along Australia's east coast sand plains once covered by water were winnowed by the winds and carried inland. Off Queensland's south coast the frantic energy of the glacial times created the sand island's greatest era of dune building activity.

The oldest dunes on Fraser Island have been dated at 400 000 years old. The second major burst of dune building took place in the windy spells of the 'little ice ages' over the last 10 000 years which succeeded the great glacial epochs. During the interglacials, when temperatures were much like today's, the sea levels were high and, like today, the sand was carried to the sea floor and delivered to the beach by the sea where the wind carried it inland. The island and its neighbouring coastal sand masses represent significant stages in the evolutionary history of the earth.

Subtle changes to the huge sandcastle that is Fraser Island are forever being wrought by the winds and tides. Differences to the island's surface have been recorded since Europeans first sailed past it 200 years ago. In the journal of his voyage along Australia's east coast in 1770 Captain Cook noted a few still-living green trees growing in a vast strand of sand on the island near Indian Head and commented that the sand must have only recently moved. The strand was the Wungul sandblow and its development and path inland have been measured since.

Cyclones wreak dramatic changes to the sand islands. By demonstrating the effects of these seasonal wild storms scientists have a unique opportunity to relate what happens to the landscape in a few weeks or months to the patterns of the past. Fraser Island is therefore an important laboratory where emerging discoveries point the way for researchers elsewhere.

A LANDSCAPE ON THE MOVE

A LANDSCAPE ON THE MOVE

The sand dunes of Fraser Island are the blueprints of the great sandcastle. Time is the architect, the sands are the building blocks and the winds are the tools. Like any sandcastle built on the beach, Fraser Island grew in stages. Piling successively one over another the dunes roll westward in series of folds across the island. The youngest, constantly replenished by raw materials from the sea, are along the ocean coastline; the oldest are in the west. The shifting sands are dynamic, forever pushed by the winds, enveloping and overlaying, the potent force controlling everything on the island.

Previous page: The struggle for survival on Fraser Island is controlled by sand – it is the dynamic factor governing all life.

The dunes are aligned with the onshore winds and are formed into a pattern of ridges running from south east to north west. Their peak is a backbone of high sand hills in the centre. Over time the dunes have succumbed to weathering. Wind, rain and erosion shave off rough edges, plane down sharp ridges, fill in furrows but the overlaying pattern is still visible. The shape is one of the pieces in the jigsaw picture of the age of the dunes. Another clue comes from comparisons with coastal sand deposits in South Australia and Victoria. Fraser Island's oldest dunes are at least 400 000 years old.

The plants growing on the dunes are also signposts to the past. The first pioneer plants survived sea journeys and gained a foothold in the sands above the beach. Gradually the vegetation established a stabilising cover, helping the dunes resist erosion and allowing further vegetation to build up. Over hundreds of thousands of years nature's handiwork has wrought subtle, unseen changes beneath the surface. The plants dropped their leaves to form rich belts in the sand able to sustain even more vegetation and gradually they provided for the abundant diversity of plants on the island.

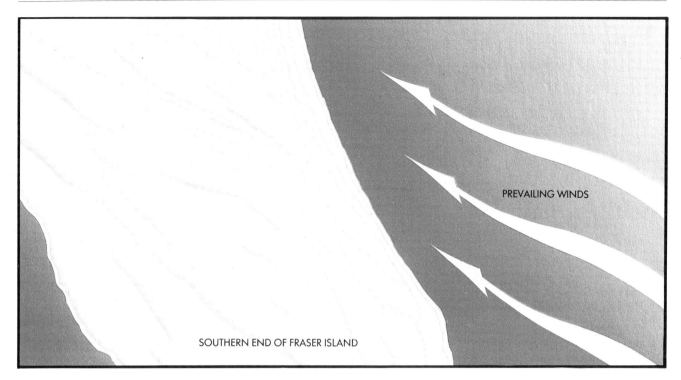

PREVAILING WINDS

SOUTHERN END OF FRASER ISLAND

Maps of soil landscapes are another means of dating the dunes and revealing how they overlay one another.

Scientists have separated the dunes into a number of types which they have labelled systems, each characterised by distinctive features. They are unable to agree on the number of systems but it is generally accepted that there are six easily identifiable types of dune. Each was laid down in distinct and different phases but all began as sand washed ashore onto the ocean beaches. Blown inland the sands formed in the shape of a parabola, a huge U-shaped scoop moulded from sand with its opening towards the sea in the direction of the prevailing winds. The term parabola was first used in 1894 to describe U-shaped sand dunes along the coast of Denmark.

From the air the parabolic shape can be seen easily. The sides of the scoop are like an enormous hairpin open to the east and tapering to an apex. On either side are trailing arms which have steep, external slopes. The interior walls incline to a hollowed-out valley. Water attacks the mobile sands and gullies and channels excavate the dune floor. What we see today has been influenced by the configuration of the

Dunes across Fraser Island form in the direction of prevailing winds.

A series of lakes has formed in the scoops gouged out of the parabolic dunes as the sands moved across the island.

underlying base sands, the initial size of the huge scoop, the effects of wind in its development and the amount of water scouring the surface and breaching the trailing arms.

The youngest dunes are sharply ridged; behind them are the crested humps of dune system two where shrubs and bigger trees expose an open canopy to the sky; they give way to the rugged dunes of the commercial forests – dune system three – where trees like the blackbutt are logged. The island's high country is dune system four, the zone of the rainforest giants. In some places the peaks are 240 metres above sea level

and creek beds cut through the forest. The vegetation is so thick it is second only to California's sequoia forests. Further west the dunes of system five begin to show their great age. They are worn into whalebacks and the vegetation is sparse. The great grandfather sand hills of the island's west coast, dune system six, are bowed down by antiquity, subdued by age with no trace of their original form. They slope gently down to the sea and their sands drift in wisps onto the beach.

Sandblows are sand dunes in the making, living laboratories where the interminable processes creating

Above: Mirrored in the lake at its head, the Lake Wabby sandblow is swallowing the waters as it gradually surges inland.

Below left: A massive wall of sand on the march. Lake Wabby is being engulfed by a sandblow at the rate of about two metres a year. In time the lake will be obliterated.

Below right: A break in the vegetation can start a sandblow. Fingers of sand reach into the foredunes and, fuelled by wind, gain momentum to spill over the landscape. Sandblows are dunes in the making.

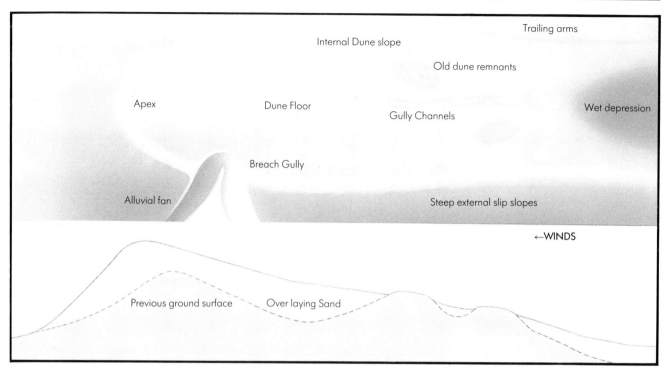

Internal Dune slope

Trailing arms

Old dune remnants

Apex

Dune Floor

Wet depression

Gully Channels

Breach Gully

Alluvial fan

Steep external slip slopes

←WINDS

Previous ground surface — Over laying Sand

Parabolic dunes

the dunes are telescoped in time. They are places of mystery, great swathes of sand forcing their way inland inexorably to engulf the landscape. They have occurred for as long as the island has been in existence and the progress of blows on the island has been measured since the appearance of Europeans. Patches of sand observed by Banks on Cook's expedition in 1770 had moved inland when Flinders noted them thirty-two years later. Banks recorded that 'we could see through our glasses that the sands which lay in great patches in many acres each were moveable; some of them had lately moved, for trees which stood up in the middle of them were quite green, others of a longer standing had many stumps sticking out of them which had been killed by the sands heaping about their roots.' In 1802 Flinders confirmed the presence of 'extensive bare patches'. The Lake Wabby sandblow is moving forward at the rate of two to three metres each year, gradually swallowing the lake at its head.

Sandblows are blowouts in the landscape occurring when a break in the vegetation leaves a cleared passage for windblown sand to exploit. Most sandblows start along the ocean coastline where the front line of plants gripping the foredunes is most vulnerable to the ravages of the wild winds of storms and cyclones.

Fires, the brumbies tearing gaps in the vegetation, paths, four-wheel-drive vehicle tracks, campsites — belonging to Aborigines in the past and, more recently, to visitors — any places where the scrub has been cleared are potential causes of sandblows.

Winds charge across the beach whipping up sand grains which are hurled like razor-sharp shards of glass to slash and uproot the plants and blast a path through the scrub. The foredune sands are released to spill over the landscape. Like a slow motion tidal wave the huge volume of sand overwhelms everything in its path. Trees and plants are engulfed in its forward surge; entire forests are suffocated under millions of tonnes of sand. Some sandblows have a face of more than fifty metres and they can run up on existing dunes to a height of 250 metres.

On little hillocks trees struggle for life, isolated like little islands of green in a sea of sand until they, too, are smothered. Fingers of sand stretch into the vegetation and, along the blow's front edge, walls of sand, sometimes as high as forty metres,

are driven onward. The wind moulds and sculpts the body of sand into craters and curves, waves, ripples and undulations of extraordinary beauty.

In the scoured wake of the blow skeletons of trees buried centuries before are exhumed; they are stark, bleached pointers to the blow's long progress. Bands of ancient sands and embedded layers of leaf litter from the original forests are exposed as the debris of past ages. Aboriginal middens and campsites with evidence of stone tools have also been uncovered. Some of the sandblows have Aboriginal names like Badjala, Nulla, Beiral and Gulbun; others are European like Knifeblade, Hammerstone, and Stonetool.

If the advancing wall of sand meets a hollow its progress may be slowed and the plants have a chance of creeping back over the edges, sometimes densely enough to stabilise the body of sand and halt its progress. Tiny seedlings push boldly through the sand and others follow. In time nature redresses the balance. Insidiously the new plants begin their reclamation. The forests crawl back over the lip of the blow. Sandblows with woody vegetation across the foot slow down to a metre or less a year. The sandblow's

Trees, long ago buried upright, are exhumed as the sand's passage continues and are left as stark pointers to the past.

enormous energy is relinquished to the robust force of vegetation.

Melaleucas, commonly called paperbarks or teatrees, are known as the great survivors in this moving landscape. Their name comes from the Greek words for black and white, the slim white trunks being topped with bunches of dark foliage. Some are estimated to be about 2000 years old, the oldest trees in Queensland.

They cannot be dated accurately by carbon dating methods because they are living organisms; the living tissues in their cells are constantly being replaced. They are able to hold their heads above the encroaching

Above: These plants are doomed. They are being suffocated as the sand forces onward.

Below: The melaleucas are the great survivors in the sand environment. They thrive in the wake of the sandblows.

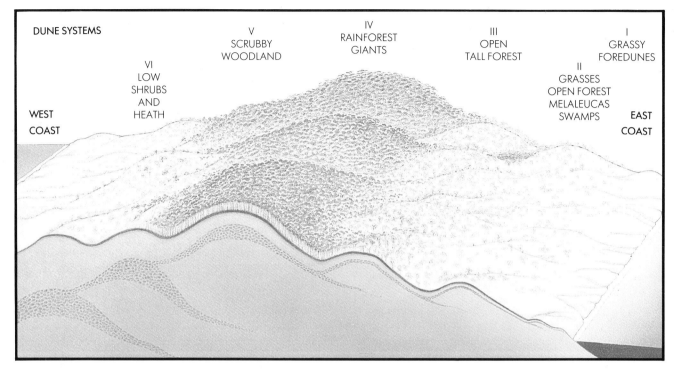

DUNE SYSTEMS

V
SCRUBBY
WOODLAND

IV
RAINFOREST
GIANTS

III
OPEN
TALL FOREST

I
GRASSY
FOREDUNES

VI
LOW
SHRUBS
AND
HEATH

II
GRASSES
OPEN FOREST
MELALEUCAS
SWAMPS

WEST
COAST

EAST
COAST

Cross section of the island showing the relationship between the vegetation on the six overlapping dune systems and the soil horizons which have formed in the sand. Near the surface the A1 horizon forms from accumulated leaf litter; below it is the A2 layer of pale sands leached by rain and, deep underground, organic compounds and mineral coatings from the sand grains have been carried to settle in the B horizon.

sand by putting down roots from their stems. In some places where the sands have moved on the melaleucas are disclosed with long streamers of roots hanging alongside their trunks. The *Melaleuca quiquinervia,* the cajeput tree, is a remarkably hardy plant and likes to grow with its feet in water. It has its own water supply in pockets in its wafer-thin layer of bark. It is abundant around Fraser Island's lakes and in the swamps. It is common in other countries. The Hong Kong Government planted melaleucas to stabilise areas of the New Territories and in Florida they are threatening

to take over part of the famous Everglades. The Queensland and Fraser Island Aborigines used the melaleucas in various ways: oil from crushed leaves was a cure for coughs, and blossoms, rich in nectar, were soaked in water for a sweet drink.

Plants also start to steal back into the excavation zone in the tracks of the sandblow where the water table is just below the surface. Vegetation re-establishes at about the same rate as the blow's movement forward. At the foot of the Lake Wabby blow every step back from the front line of the colonising plants represents a year in the age of the plants there.

Among the forerunner plants are the dogwoods, sheoaks (casuarinas) and wattles (acacias) such as the Brisbane black wattle.

A scant lacework of animals' footprints is brief testimony to the transitory passage of animals across the dunes. For some the vast expanses of the sandblows are hunting grounds; their shelters are along the fringes of the blow. The sands record the passage of reptiles – skinks, lizards, goannas, geckos and snakes, small mammals like native mice, bandicoots and wallabies. The large footprints of the predator dingo etch patterns across the dunes – footprints in the sands of time.

A JOURNEY IN TIME

A JOURNEY IN TIME

The landscape is one of high wooded forests, dense scrub, thickets of wildflowers, tangled rainforest vines, ferns and palms among tall trees reaching to the sky, verdant swamps and grasslands and that all these thrive on sand is one of Fraser Island's greatest wonders. The island is a flourishing botanic paradise; the huge sandheap is the matrix for a thriving and complex ecology. How can the sand support all these plants?

A journey across the island traverses half a million years of botanical history. The sand and the plants have developed links so that each dune phase supports a different type of vegetation. Soil begins to develop as leaf litter decays and minerals from the sand form a fertile layer under the surface. Time's work on the sand has created well-defined bands – the soil horizons. What is happening beneath the dunes is paralleled by the plants on each system. The plant communities are mirrors of the thickness of the fertile layers.

Soil development in the dunes begins with the first colonising plants and proceeds under a vegetative cover, increasing as it advances inland to reach its thickest layers under the rainforests of type four dunes. There are four major factors in the build-up of soils: the amount of moisture falling as rain and percolating through the ground; the rate at which erosion takes place; the recycling of organic matter from the plants themselves; and the length of time the sands are subjected to weathering.

The sand grains are the first source of plant nutriments. Grains washed ashore and blown onto the beaches are the unweathered 'virgin' sands, quartz grains which get their pale yellow-brown colour from coatings of aluminium and iron oxides. Minute quantities of other minerals encase the grains like nacre around pearls – calcium, magnesium, potassium phosphorous and sulphur as well as traces of zinc and molyb-

Previous page: Sturdy colonisers of the island's shoreline, grass seeds gain a hold in the sands above the beach, paving the way for flourishing plant communities.

denum. They are all precious to the plants. Rainwater releases the minerals and they are snapped up by the plants' roots. In turn, the plants drop their leaves to litter the ground; rain and moisture do their work, recycling the wastes into rich humus.

In addition the plants grab all they can from the air. Windblown dust particles and, along the coast, fallout from seaspray contribute nutriment supplies in what is called atmospheric accession. Concentrations of elements such as calcium, potassium and magnesium are high along the ocean coast, where the beach is often misty with seaspray, and diminish progressively inland. Five hundred metres from the beach the concentrations drop by half and then decline less rapidly. But the sea breezes can be foe as well as friend to plants along the shore. Too much salt is destructive and plants near the sea have their own ways of coping with it. Spinifex grass has fine hairs, and pigface and convolvulus have tough fleshy leaves to protect them from excess salt (and from the burning temperatures of the sand, too). Some sheoaks collect a briny mixture in the night dew in pockets behind their leaves. Other kinds of sheoak hang their leafy curtains to protect the plants behind them; how-

ever, some, like the banksias (bottlebrushes) and acacias (wattles) of the coast are pruned by the salty winds.

If plants further inland cannot rely on atmospheric accession they have to get their nutriments by other means. One way they do this is with the aid of fungi. Plants colonising mobile sandblows in the rainforest and bare sand near the beach use fungi dwelling in the sand to mobilise mineral nutriments on the individual grains. The fungi stretch out fine, microscopic, hair-like threads known as hyphae, to which the sand grains cling.

The hyphae enfold the plants' roots and moisture is trapped, releasing minerals around the grains to be absorbed by the roots. Sand grains clinging to long strings of hyphae can be seen like tiny necklaces just under the surface and around the roots of plants. They have been found in thick clusters, up to four metres of hyphae in a millilitre of sand. Curtains of hyphae and their attached grains of sand also hang from banks eroded in the dunes. The close associations between the roots and the hyphae are called mycorrhizas. Because the fungus has no chlorophyl and cannot synthesise for itself the roots supply

Plants and fungi have forged bonds to extract nutriments from the sand. An eroded bank reveals hairlike strands of fungi, called hyphae, which trap grains and bring them into contact with the roots of plants.

various organic compounds to it, an interaction which is a symbiotic relationship necessary for both the fungi and the plants. Orchid growers use this connection and it also operates in forests of northern Europe where the cold inhibits the breakdown of pine needles into humus and fungi assist in releasing chemical substances for the trees.

Fungal hyphae can exist without their associated plants only when they are producing spores. Scientists have measured threads of hyphae in the bare sand of sandblows up to six metres ahead of the colonising plants. Mats of hyphae enmesh the

sand grains and help stabilise the dunes by making the surface water-repellant and less vulnerable to erosion. This most useful function is being investigated as a means of re-vegetating bare sand dunes, not only on Fraser Island, but in other places where erosion and mining have stripped the sands of their protective blankets of plants.

Layers of sands beneath the surface are soil horizons, each a zone of distinctly different characteristics which scientists examine by drilling cores to learn the profile of each layer. Build-up of soil is constant and continuous; it is part of the process governed by the sands and has been taking place since the first grass seed was carried ashore by the surf and settled in the sand above the beach.

Most of the nutriments extracted by the plants from the sand return to collect on the ground as a litter of leaves, twigs and bark. Micro-organisms get to work on the litter and convert it to humus, a dark, enriched layer on the surface called the A 1 horizon. Rain, seeping through the sand, picks up the organic compounds and the mineral coatings around the sand grains and carries them deeper into the dunes, leaving behind a belt of sand denuded of its colouring and nutriments. This is the pale, leached A 2 horizon. Where the humus and minerals accumulate deep in the sands, a layer, stained yellow-brown, settles. This is the B horizon. Soils formed by precipitation this way in areas of temperate, humid climates like Fraser Island's are called podsols. They are the zones of greatest nutriments for plants. The B horizon has another quality. Over time it can become cemented into hard lumps, crumbly like fudge and about the same colour. Patches are found scattered over the island. They are not real rocks and they are known as coffee rock or humate. Along the beaches the blackened lumps are worn smooth by the waves and are called sandrock.

Time is the secret component in the underground story of soils. Thousands of years have leached the B horizon deeper and deeper into the dunes. The vegetation on each dune system is a clue to what is happening beneath the surface. From the east coast across the older dunes to the peak in the rainforest of system four, plant cover increases according to depth of nutriment. Nature has devised a simple formula: the thicker the leaves, the greater the nutriments to support more plants which can grow to

Seams of decayed plant matter, hardened over thousands of years into coffee rock or humate, are exposed along the west coast where the sand from the island's oldest dunes falls in wisps to the sea.

greater heights. Vegetation on the dunes acts as windows in the time gradient of forest succession. Soil profiles across the dunes tell their own story. In the youngest dunes, the B horizon is about 40 cm to 50 cm deep; in system two it is between 50 and 70 centimetres; in three, from 90 to 120 centimetres; in four, from 3.7 metres to 8 metres. In system five it falls rapidly to between 12 and 16 metres and, finally, the huge profiles of system six along the west coast show the B horizon up to 25 metres underground. Wind and water scouring chunks from the ancient dunes along the inland shore have prepared a geology lesson for all to see. In some places where erosion has sliced off sections from the cliffs, the giant profiles are visible.

Crossing from the lush rainforests to the sparse heathland of the old whaleback hills on their western flanks is like stepping across a time zone into another country. The two areas may be separated by only a few metres yet the difference is stark. In the lee of the rainforest grottoes the scrub is dwarfed; it is growing in a different time zone and its shrubs, thrusting out of the sand, are straggling and twisted.

Hundreds of thousands of years have been at work on these oldest dunes. The productive layers, buried far beneath the surface, are covered by a thick blanket of sand stripped white, its minerals leached far underground. Time has taken the B horizon out of reach of the plants' roots; none can stretch as far as twenty-five metres. The plants have to scrape what they can from the depleted soils and from their own scattered leaf litter as it decomposes on the surface. Sheltered from the breezes of the ocean they miss out on most of the airborne nutriments as well. Only the hardiest varieties struggle into the sunlight. The banksias, stringy barks and shallow-rooting flowering shrubs are the tough battlers of this environment. Some of the yellow flowering native peas can handle the conditions; they produce rich levels of nitrogen and return it to the soil. At any month of the year wildflowers carpet the island with the best months being in spring. In August and September the dry heathland of the west is transformed under a mantle of colour. The bush is alive with yellow and mauve, purple and pink, cream and white, a bright patchwork of variety and texture.

Scientists in the last decade have probed with drills and peered through microscopes to discover facts about the fascinating relationship between Fraser Island's soils and plant communities which have opened up new realms for their colleagues in other parts of the world. Their findings have challenged a theory known as Plant Climax. Until recently botanists believed that for every undisturbed site in the world there is a pattern in the progression of vegetation. They took their guide from places like the forests of northern Europe where they studied the effects of the climate, the lie of the land, the age of the soils and so on. They investigated the types of plants that succeed one another in a chang-

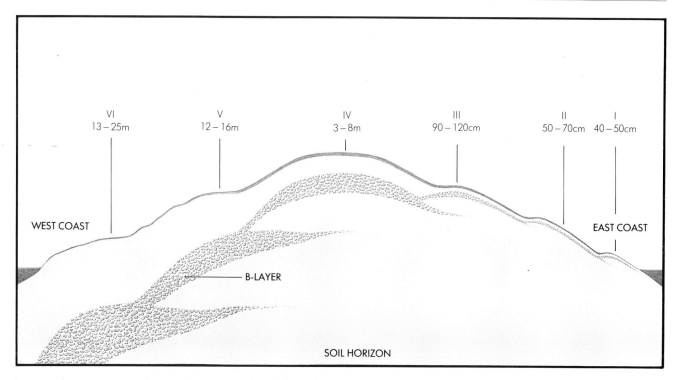

VI
13 – 25m

V
12 – 16m

IV
3 – 8m

III
90 – 120cm

II
50 – 70cm

I
40 – 50cm

WEST COAST

EAST COAST

B-LAYER

SOIL HORIZON

ing environment such as the edges of lakes that were gradually drying up or former pastures being resumed by native vegetation. They concluded that plant communities in such places succeed one another until they reach a climax, a final, ultimate botanical state perpetuated by the plants themselves by recycling what they take from the ground from their own wastes. This theory was put to use in managing native forests and predicting how woodlands would develop after their environments were disturbed.

The theory was based on findings from the relatively young, post glac-ial landscapes of the northern hemis-phere. It had not reckoned on the effects of prolonged erosion on the ancient soils in Australia's – and Fraser Island's – coastal dunes which started to form after they were laid down in the Great Ice Ages. Because Australian scientists have been able to map the evolution of the dunes and the links with the plants growing on them, climax has been shown to be only a passing phase; in time most ecosystems will disintegrate. Fraser Island's rainforest giants are only the middle of the story; the stunted dwarfs of the ancient dunes give a hint of the ending.

Soil horizons across the dunes. The thickness of the vegetation matches the underground strands of the nutritive-rich B horizon.

TREASURES IN THE SAND

TREASURES IN THE SAND

One hundred and twelve kilometres long, pounded endlessly by waves, Fraser Islands's ocean beach hides a glory box of treasures. The beach holds the gift of life, the stretch of sand nurtures, nourishes and protects hundreds of creatures. Some find their food in the sand, some live beneath it. For some, like the globe-wandering migratory birds and the flocks of terns, the beach is a resting place and its wave-washed sands are their feeding grounds.

Along one third of the shoreline the spectacular cliffs of coloured sands rise like bulwarks from the beach, the sea scuffing their foundations at high tide. The surf refreshes pools formed in crevices among the rocky headlands. Between Indian Head and Middle Rocks a large pool known as the Aquarium shelters fish and other sea life. From the headland one looks down into its blue depths sometimes to see a shark trapped there, waiting for the next high tide to carry it back out to sea. From this vantage point the sandy shoals of the island's northern promontory spread their swirls of colour – turquoise and aqua to deep sea greens, ultramarine and indigo. Bottlenose dolphins play in the waves and sometimes whales plough along the coast and sea birds swoop and dive. Occasionally big sea turtles are washed ashore, but the surf is too strong for them to come onto the island's beaches to lay their eggs. Their breeding grounds are off Sandy Cape and sometimes the currents carry them into the Great Sandy Strait. The turtles' breeding season lasts from mid-November until January.

The sandy beach may appear deserted to the casual observer, but it is teeming with life. At low tide the sand bubbler crabs come up in thousands from their subterranean habitat to feed and transform the beaches with the debris of their twice daily foraging. They are sievers

Previous page: The sands of time – key to the secrets of Fraser Island.

of plankton, the drifting and floating life of the ocean brought in with each wave, and the eaters of the detritus, the disintegrating debris of the sea. They work urgently, sifting the sand grains and sorting out the organic bits and pieces to swallow. The cleaned sand is formed into balls to be rejected and rolled backwards through their tunnel of legs to fan behind them. The incoming tide puts an end to feeding. The crabs disappear back underground, leaving the beach with patches of sand pellets radiating from their holes.

There are crabs at every level of the beach. Deep in the soft sand above the high tide mark the ghost crabs make their burrows, sometimes up to a metre underground. Tiny tracks lead to the entrances. At twilight the crabs come out to forage in the wet sand at low tide and if they are disturbed they will elude capture by running into the sea.

But they are mostly land creatures and very fleet of foot. The ghost crabs are well named; their translucent sand colour with traces of pink and yellow gives them excellent concealment against the sand.

Other scavengers of the tiny particles of debris are the giant beach worms which live completely hidden in the sand. Their diet includes decaying debris as well as live flesh. The Aborigines in past centuries knew about this habit and it has been utilised by today's fishermen. A piece of rotting fish or meat drawn above the wet sand is a signal to the worms underneath, attracting them to the surface. Heads pop up to grab the lure but the worm catcher needs to be quick. He must grasp the worm's head firmly and draw it smoothly from the sand. The skilled practitioner is well rewarded; the worms can grow to more than a metre in length and make fine bait. The Aborigines developed this skill to a fine art.

They were also expert at feeling out another dweller of the sandy shores – the pipis, the young of which are also victims of the giant beach worm. The pipis are eugaries, known to the Fraser Islanders as 'wongs' and were favoured food of the Aborigines. Their midden sites are scattered with wong shells from long-ago feasts. The shellfish make excellent bait and fishermen still use the time-honoured methods of treading the wet sands with bare feet for the tell tale lumps under the surface which indicate the presence of the wongs.

As the tide approaches low water mark scores of pairs of tiny holes appear in the sand. A wave washes

Above: The water's edge is a rendezvous for crested terns. They preen, rest, flirt and, with delicacy and astonishing brevity, they mate.

Below: A dolphin at play in the surf off the ocean beach.

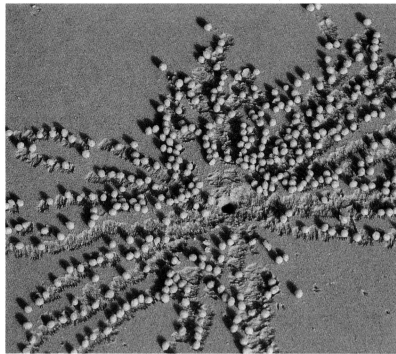

in and recedes, leaving what look like dozens of shining pebbles. But these are the wongs which open their winged shells, push out their fleshy feet and turn the shells on end, pulling them down by the feet into the safety of the sand. The performance is incredibly fast and is made by the young pipis who feed nearer the surface than the older, larger pipis. They cannot be seen and a sensitive set of toes is the best means of locating them.

The experts among the pipi catchers are the island's pied oyster catchers. Smart-looking black and white birds with strong red legs, beaks and

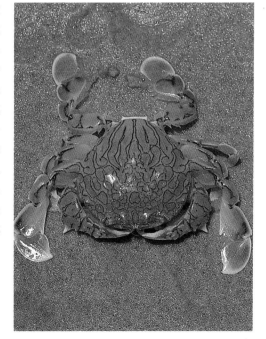

Above left: At low tide the sand bubbler crab comes to the surface to feed. Sieving food particles from the sand grains with amazing dexterity, it forms the discarded grains into balls and rejects them through the tunnel of its legs.

Above right: Pellets of sand radiate from a sand bubbler's hole, and, as the tide turns, the beach is strewn with the remnants of its feeding.

Below: A tracery of patterns on its shell gives the double-lined sand crab its name. Oar-like paddles on its feet make the crab an efficient digger and swimmer.

eyes, they work in pairs probing the sand with vertically-flattened beaks that are hammer-hard. The feeding pipi below the surface is open: the beak thrusts inside and the pipi attempts to snap shut, but it closes its shell on the beak. The oyster catchers are very deft. Withdrawing the pipi they lever it open and scissor it off its shell for a succulent meal. Bird watchers and fishermen have reported seeing patches of the beach scrabbled by the birds' footprints and scattered with the fresh shells of open pipis. They surmise that the oyster catchers bring some of the shellfish to the surface and leave them to open in the sun.

Pied oyster catchers are found year round on the island, making the stretch of Seventy Mile Beach one of their favourite spots. They lay their eggs in shallow depressions among the grasses and vines clinging to the dry sand just above the beach. Their open nests are vulnerable to predators: dingoes scavenging along the foredunes and birds of prey like brahminy kites and sea eagles take their toll of the next season's youngsters. When danger threatens the parents will try the broken wing trick: dragging one wing limply along the ground and calling their loud, rather melancholy cry, they attempt to distract the intruder. The eggs hatch in spring and although the fluffy cream and brown chicks are well camouflaged by the shadows and hidden by tufts of grass they, too, are easy prey.

The piebald oyster catchers take their place on the seashore among the hordes of fishermen who throng Fraser Island's ocean beaches during the fishing season. The birds' jaunty movements as they wade in the wash, fossick for wongs on the edge of the surf, stretch and pirouette on their red legs mimic the fishermen who stand, shoulder to shoulder, in the waves.

Every year between August and October the peaceful calm of the beaches is shattered as thousands of fishermen are drawn to Fraser Island by the prospect of excellent sport during what is known as the annual tailor run. The visitors come in four-wheel-drive vehicles, turning the long ocean beach into a busy highway.

Vehicles laden with all the comforts of home make the barge-crossing from the mainland and tent cities appear along the foredunes. As well as their rods and lines the fishermen bring electric generators for lighting and power and their huge freezers gradually fill with catches to be

Above: Year-round inhabitants of the ocean shore, pied oyster catchers fossick for food in the waves in pairs and nest in the grasses and vines matting the foredunes.

Below: A fluffy oyster catcher chick needs its sandy colouring as a protection from predators as it shelters near a crevice in the foredunes.

enjoyed later. Washing hangs from tent guy ropes and dogs and children play in the wavelets. The fishing folk are usually an amiable lot – they are on holidays and in relaxed mood. In the last ten years since the island and its attractions have become better known, visitors from the southern states have joined the annual fishing bonanza. Easter and school holidays also bring large crowds.

Crabs scuttle for cover, brumbies gaze mournfully from the foredunes at the scenes of camp activity and sea birds fight for titbits as fish are cleaned on the beach. Fishing is considered good at all times of the year with plenty of dart, flathead, bream and whiting, but the tailor, sought at low tide in gutters in the breakers and off the headlands are the most highly prized.

The tailor is pelagic (living close to the ocean's surface) and is a strong fighting fish which can swim fast. The tailor bites readily and gives the fisherman good sport. It is an excellent eating fish, said to be the best if cut and bled as soon as it is taken from the water. The origin of its name is unknown, perhaps it is a corruption of an Aboriginal name.

Fraser Island is the most northerly point for tailor. They come in huge schools from waters as far south as Victoria to spawn in the strip of ocean between Indian Head and Sandy Cape. Then they disappear. Fisheries services have conducted tagging programs but the full story of why the fish behave this way is still not known.

The number and size of catches has been decreasing steadily in the last few years, due, some say, to the increasing numbers of visitors. One regular visitor who has been going to the island for twenty-five years reported that in 1984 the drop in the tailor catch was dramatic. That season more dart, whiting and bream were taken than tailor even though a few years ago tailor was the predominant fish caught during the three-month season. He echoes the concern of many people that the rising numbers of visitors are exacting a high price from the island and that its delicate and fragile state needs protection to prevent its misuse. The only fishing limit is minimum size, not number.

The fishermen link up to the beach telegraph through CB radios and congregate in places along the beach when word goes out that 'the fish are running'. A few years ago to catch a 4.5 kilogram tailor was common; nowadays a fish half that weight is considered good.

Twelve years ago the island received about 1000 visitors a year; there has been an increase of almost fifty per cent each year since then. Not all come for the fishing. The Forestry Department at Central Station has kept figures of visitor numbers. In March, 1981, 7000 people passed through the station in a three week holiday period. Today it is many more. Vehicle numbers have also increased. In 1984 1400 vehicles were recorded crossing to the island compared with 800 in 1981 and 400 in 1979.

The lines of fishermen in the surf, colourful in their bright yellow waterproof clothing, their modern vehicles drawn up on the beach and with elaborate paraphernalia are a far cry from the Aborigines and their simple fishing methods of the past. Where they relied on dolphin out at sea to alert them to schools of fish, the fishermen today have their radio sets. The Aborigines' scoop nets woven from bark have been replaced by intricate glass fibre rods and lines. Few of today's fishermen who wander off the beaches to explore the island's hinterland would recognise the foam bark tree, *Jagera pseudorhus*, an aid to fishing the Aboriginal way. Branches of the tree were used to beat the water in freshwater creeks and streams. The leaves released a chemical which stunned the fish so they could be caught by hand. Living in harmony with their environment, the Aborigines knew the island, their provider for thousands of years.

GRASSLANDS AND SWAMPS

GRASSLANDS AND SWAMPS

Scientists have distinguished four major land systems and about twenty different plant communities on the dunes of Fraser Island. Sometimes the visitor on his trek of discovery can see the divisions that mark some of them, such as the striking contrast between the rainforest and the heathland to the west or along the edges of sandblows where colonising plants are marching back over the sand, but mostly time-weathering, erosion and the effects of fire have masked the more obvious signs.

Previous page: Silent and brooding, the swamps are the domain of carnivorous plants, reptiles and the enclosed world of insects.

Almost half the island is made up of low altitude dunes, open eucalypt forests, some of the sandblows and poorly-drained areas of grasses and bracken ferns. In the north are the low dunes of open woodland, heath and scrub, freshwater lakes and sandblows. The interior, the region of the highest dunes with their covering of thick forests and spectacular perched lakes, encompasses about one quarter of the island's sandy mass. About five per cent of the island's 163 000 hectares is rainforest or, more correctly, vineforest, confined almost exclusively to this central region. Finally, the wetlands and lowlands, lagoons and swamps are along the west coast facing Great Sandy Strait and extending towards the southern tip of the island.

A trek on Fraser Island is an adventure dominated by plants; a treasureland supporting a varied botanical mix. It is easy to be distracted by the massive trees of the tall forests, to marvel at their splendour and to realise they are sustained by sand, but it pays to look down at the myriad small plants, the ferns, grasses and shrubs that quilt the sands of this fascinating island.

Sheltered by the ridges of the foredunes from the blasting onslaught of the salty sea breezes, the plants gradually gain a hold and increase in variety and number as one travels inland. Soft breezes wafting through the feathery veils of sheoak trees set up a peaceful, murmuring hum. Their foliage consists of fine branchlets. The wood of sheoaks is hard; it was used by the Aborigines for boomerangs and other weapons. Smaller, tough shrubs such as lantana, hop bush and a kind of native citrus with shiny round leaves also grow in this zone. Celery wood – it gets its name from the foliage which, when crushed, exudes an odour like that of the familiar salad vegetable – and the quinine berry, which produces an attractive but bitter-tasting fruit inducing a raging thirst, are other interesting plants of this zone.

The bushland is noisy with birdsong. Flocks of pigeons such as topknots, wompoo and red-crowned, make their gentle cooing calls to a background of the shriller notes of birds like honeyeaters, robins, swallows, whistlers and flycatchers.

More than 300 species of bird have been recorded on Fraser Island, its neighbouring sand islands and the coastal fringe, more species than in the British Isles. Of these about 200 are land birds drawn by the prolific plant life of the region. There are no species endemic to the island although for many it is the boundary of their habitat.

The shy ground parrot, one of Australia's rare species, has been found on Fraser Island in small numbers. It is restricted to areas of low heath country. The island and nearby Cooloola are the northern limit of its range in eastern Australia. The area is also the northern limit for other birds including the brush bronzewing, the white-cheeked honey eater and the little wattle bird. Fraser Island also appears to be the southernmost range for other birds including the large-tailed nightjar, the barn swallow, the shining flycatcher and the dusky honeyeater.

Other birds with a predominantly inland distribution recorded on the island include the red-winged parrot, red-backed honeyeater, singing bushlark, Australian raven and the square-tailed kite which can be found scavenging on the beaches or in the hinterland where it preys on other, smaller birds and steals eggs from their nests.

The gorgeous rainbow-bird is well named. Slim and graceful with a long curved tail and two elongated tail feathers, its back is a glossy turquoise and it has a pale orange throat. Its flight is swift and soaring. Fraser Island suits it well as it builds its nest in chambers in the sand, tunnelling burrows sometimes up to a

Above: The iridescent plumage of the rainbow-bird, or bee-eater, is a flash of colour in the bush.

Below: Vivid emerald foxtail sedges wave their feathery fronds in the sun.

Opposite: Crystal balls of death. The sticky globules of the carnivorous plant, Drosera binata, entrap unwary insects which are succulent prey for the plant and its partner assassin bug. The bug is immune to the plant's fatal attractions.

metre long where four or five white, shiny eggs are laid. The mating pair take it in turns at digging, they rest on exposed branches to launch themselves at passing prey. The rainbow-bird's food is insects and it is also known as the bee-eater. Often, before mating, the male will bring his mate the gift of an insect. The birds roost in flocks among the mangroves and amidst the rainforest canopy.

Fraser Island and Great Sandy Strait are the resting places for migratory birds which land from April to October each year after their long ocean flight from the Bering Sea and

on their return a few months later. Some remain on the island during summer and many immature birds may stay there longer. The island is an important resting place for Mongolian sand plovers which breed in Siberia, eastern curlews and bar-tailed godwits which haunt the tidal flats and estuaries of the western foreshores. In the pink glow of sunset waves of birds wheeling and keeling over the waters of Great Sandy Strait are among the island's most beautiful and memorable sights. Surveys of migratory birds are contributing to an international study which includes Japan, China, Alaska, South Korea and New Zealand.

Encircled by copses of shrubs like lantana, boronia and trees such as brush and soap box, dogwoods, banksias and wattles are swamps, patches where the water table meets the ground level. The bungwal fern grows around the swamps. Its underground root-like stems, or rhizomes, were a staple food for the Aborigines. Pandanus crouch above thickets of ferns, marsh grasses, mosses, vines and bright emerald green foxtail sedges. Water the colour of pewter collects to mirror clumps of reeds.

In the strange, sinister world of the swamps nature has created an extraordinary union of plants and animals struggling to extract the means of life from the sand. The swamps may look deserted and desolate but a close look reveals a miniature battle being fought between life and death. The swamps are the territory of the carnivorous plants where water has leached most of the nitrogen out of the sand. The plants supplement their needs by catching insects. The carnivorous plants of Fraser Island are sundews, members of the *Drosera* family of which there are about ninety species throughout the world, many of them growing in the bogs and peaty soils of Western Australia. They trap the insects in sticky substances and convert the creatures' fluids for their own use. The forked sundew is a fern-like herb common in the swamps and around the shores of lakes on the island. It has white flowers and long narrow leaves the blades of which are segmented into forked branches. It was the plant chosen by Charles Darwin for his experiments on carnivorous plants. The *Drosera lovellae* is a native of Fraser Island. It is a small, deep red prostrate plant which dots the damp white sand fringes of the lakes and the swamps. It was named after schoolmistress Shirley Lovell.

The leaves are the operative parts of the sundews. They unfold from buds like the fronds of a fern and are covered on the upper side with sticky glands which glisten with a drop of clear, viscous fluid containing enzymes which act on the flesh of the captured insect. The plant absorbs the juice, rich with nitrogenous and mineral nutriments.

The forked sundew has a mate, a partner insect which can avoid the plant's fatal attractions. It is an assassin bug of the blood and juice-sucking insects. It camps on the back of the leaf and sucks the vital fluids from the captured prey. The bug is the housekeeper in this harmonious relationship; it cleans up the debris, leaving the sundew waiting to entice its next victim.

Tufts of green, knife-pointed spears of grasstrees swathe parts of the grasslands of the open forests. Ancient plants, they grow slowly and often require the heat of a bushfire to prompt flowering. Remnants of grasstree butts from the coastal margin of the mainland have been estimated as growing more than 35 000 years ago. The rigid leaves of grasstrees shoot in a clump from a stubby stem rough with the bases of old leaves, and tiny, star-shaped flowers spring from a long spike in the centre of the crown. On Fraser Island the grasstrees average about two metres in height, stunted in comparison with their cousins in other parts of Australia where they can reach more than twice that height. Heat causes resin to exude from the trunk and this was once a valuable source of a special sort of gum used in making varnishes, glues and floor polishes in Australia. The resin from grasstrees was a valuable ingredient for lacquer and for the outside of food tins, and during World War Two the resin found its way into munitions laboratories as a binder and fuel. Collection of grasstree resin has now stopped.

The flowers have always attracted insects to their strongly scented nectar and some creatures use grasstrees as nurseries. The carpenter bee, a spectacular, solitary insect, has a bright blue abdomen and is Australia's largest bee. It bores a hole in the dried, hollow stalks of last season's leaves and tunnels a series of about eight cells, using fragments of pith and saliva for walls to seal each cell. In each a mixture of nectar and pollen is deposited, food for the larvae when they hatch.

The carpenter bee is vegetarian, the digger wasp is a predator and,

Above: Its spotted cape raised in self defence, the frilled-neck lizard pauses during its dash to safety across the dunes.

Below: The forest floor is the hunting ground of the pink tongued skink. Its strong jaws have latched onto a land snail.

like the bee, its preparations for the next generation are elaborate and fascinating. The wasp makes its nurseries in the sand in chambers at the end of underground branched passages. In each the wasp places a stock of food for the larvae when they hatch. Each kind of wasp selects a different sort of insect as prey, such as a plant-sucking bug or a caterpillar, and paralyses it with a sting so that the food source for its young remains alive but unable to move. The larvae gradually eat the captured prey until, finally, when the vital parts are consumed, the wasp's victims die.

Above: An insect falls prey to a young frilled-neck lizard.

Below: When alarmed, its jaws open and its scaly 'beard' erect, the bearded dragon resembles a prehistoric monster.

Scurrying through the dunes are scores of different kinds of ant: more than 300 species have been found in the coastal sand mass where their distribution depends on such things as temperature, food supply, shade and drainage. Their contribution to aerating the sands and helping in soil development is often dramatically evident on the tracks running through the dunes where a colony's nest-building will bring yellow sand grains from below the surface to scatter the pale sands on top. Few ants live in the bare, hot, dry foredunes and few are found in the shaded, damp rainforest pockets. Ants found in rainforests are of the kind adapted to cool climates. Studying ants in the Great Sandy Region is one of the means scientists use in understanding soil development of the dunes and vegetation patterns.

Springtails are the minute creatures which get their name from the mechanism nature has provided enabling them to leap over the ground. Only a few millimetres long, springtails have a spring held by a catch on the underside of their bodies. They are found throughout the world and may make up a quarter of all the tiny invertebrates in eastern Australia's rainforest where they are an important part of the nutriment cycle. Fifty-seven species, of which five had never previously been collected, were recorded in the Great Sandy Region. Scientists found the greatest diversity of springtails in the grassy forests and suggested that different plant communities seem to support distinct varieties of these creatures. Although all of them can be found elsewhere they have made their homes on Fraser Island among the sands which dominate every aspect of life.

In many studies of the sand mass of the region the scientists have only just found the path to its secrets, but each discovery is a stride towards disclosing some of the mysteries.

Fraser Island has its share of reptiles. Forty-six land species have been recorded, among them Australia's deadly taipan and the highly venomous death adder. Red bellied black snakes and eastern brown snakes, also with potent venom, live on the island. Green tree snakes with their brilliant lime and yellow colouring and their rapid sinuous movements have been found in the swamps and around the lakes in large numbers and the carpet python, with its distinctive mottlings, has been recorded in various locations foraging for its diet of birds and small mammals.

Australia's most numerous lizards, the skinks, are well represented with fourteen species identified on the island, including the major skinks and the eastern blue-tongue lizard which protrudes its dark blue tongue as it moves. Lace monitors are common on the island, often seen scaling trees in search of birds' eggs, as is the sand monitor, striking with its spots and streaks of pale yellow. The spectacular dragon lizards such as the bearded dragon and the frilled-neck lizard raise themselves upright onto their hind legs as they dart across the dunes. When running or alarmed, the frilled-neck lizard lifts its beautifully spotted cape around its head as a bluff.

One of Australia's primitive 'blind' snakes was found on the island.

These snakes venture out to feed at night, relying on a highly developed sense of smell to detect their prey. Their eyes are mere patches hidden beneath the scales of the head. Two species of gecko and the lance-headed lizard, a legless lizard with a sharp-pointed snout often mistaken for a snake, have also been recorded. The lance-headed lizard can produce a tiny, mouse-like squeak and is widely distributed throughout Australia.

Several species of sea snake have been collected along the east coast including ornamented and yellow-bellied sea snakes. Like most of the island's creatures, the land reptiles are seldom seen – a tracery of markings weaving over the sand is usually the only indicator of their presence.

THE TALL FORESTS

THE TALL FORESTS

Climbing from the island's low, swampy areas and grasslands towards the central range of the highest dunes the bushwalker enters the open forest of eucalypts and larger trees.

There are three layers evident in the vegetation of the dunes of system three and the overlap: the tree canopy, the shrubs and the ground cover. All of these are more varied than the area immediately behind the foredunes.

The trees are taller, their leafy crowns open to the sky. This is a zone of scribbly gums, rusty gums or smooth-barked apple gums, forest oaks and bloodwoods. Macrozamia palms, wattles and sheoaks live in the protection of the taller trees and, on the ground, bracken ferns, kangaroo grass and the barbed wire fern, ready to snare the trekker's clothing, grow on the forest floor. Scribbly gums get their name from the whorls and etchings in their smooth bark made by a small burrowing insect. They can grow to about twenty metres and are common in the south of the island yet rare in similar areas in the north. No satisfactory explanation has been given for this puzzle, another of the strange mysteries of the island. The smooth-barked apple is a member of the myrtle family which can grow to twenty metres. It has smooth, reddish bark which glows with a brilliant burnish in summer when its bunches of creamy white flowers appear. The cup-shaped fruits have given the tree its name, *Angophora*, which comes from the Greek words meaning cup-bearer. Favouring the eastern coastal sandstone country the tree is common in Queensland and New South Wales and it is also known as the Sydney red gum. Other plants of this family are the *callistemons* or bottlebrushes which attract birds and other creatures to their sweet honey nectar.

The dominant trees of these forests are described as sclerophyll plants whose tough leaves are able to withstand long periods of dryness. They were well developed in

Previous page: The huge sandheap that is Fraser Island supports tall trees and thick forests.

Australia thirty million years ago and flourished in the infertile landscapes. They gradually made their way onto the coastal land masses like Fraser Island, replacing the heathland as nutriments from the sea and the sand grains worked their way into the soils. Land connections during the various phases of Fraser Island's formation helped speed up the process. It has been estimated that the hardy plants invaded the coastal dunes and eventually the sand islands at the rate of about 120 kilometres every half a million years.

Over time nature has provided plants of the sclerophyll forests with the ability to resist the damaging effects of fire and arise from the ashes renewed. Indeed, many depend on bushfires to assist in their regeneration. But as nature ensures balance, the leaves contain minerals such as tannins, oils and resins which are highly flammable, particularly in high temperatures and after prolonged droughts. Fraser Island's high rainfall helps the trees grow again with renewed vigour after fire but sometimes it may be several years before there are enough mature trees to produce flowers, seeds and fruit. Animals which depend on these for food have trouble finding enough to survive.

One study undertaken by a scientist from the University of Queensland showed how adaptable animals can be under the pressures of the aftermath of fire. He studied the habits of a small seed and plant-eating mammal bush rat so far found on Fraser Island but on none of its neighbouring sand islands. The habitat of the animal was destroyed by a fire which swept through the trapping area halfway through the two-and-a-half-year study. After the fire the rats had to compete with ants for food. The rats' usual behaviour patterns were reversed. The female rats, normally not dominant in the colony, became more aggressive than the males in their search for food so that the young could be born healthy. Interesting speculations about the resource thresholds of animals when their habitats are disturbed resulted from this study.

Not all the forest is destroyed by fire. A few trees usually escape when natural fires, started by lightning or other natural causes, sweep through the bush. Some eucalypts, banksias, sheoaks and tea trees have thick bark insulating their stems from the heat. The crowns of the trees will be burnt but, eventually, buds buried deep in blackened stems will sprout

shoots, and in time the trees will be wearing new green vests. Other trees rely on the intense heat of bushfires to burst open and release their seeds which may have lain dormant underground for many years. Others, including members of the banksia family such as hakea and geebung and sheoaks, enclose their seeds in densely-packed cones of woody fruits for many years until the heat of fire splits them open. All these tough, hardy trees and shrubs grow in parts of the island subjected to bushfires and where the soils are depleted of nutriments such as nitrogen and phosphorous.

Control burning helps reduce the devastation of wild fires and the forestry department and the Queensland National Parks and Wildlife Service conduct such fires on Fraser Island from time to time in the cooler months. A few weeks after a fire the bush springs back to life with blackened, scorched trunks cloaked in pale green foliage.

In addition to their strategies to overcome the effects of fire some of the plants of the dunes have ways of coping with poor, depleted soils. Scribbly gums and banksias usually have three stems instead of the usual four or more found in richer soils. This means less mass for the trees to

support. They are able to sit out bad seasons by storing food in woody tubers which bulge in lumps on their trunks. Many varieties of spider flower (*grevilleas*) and banksia, members of the proteoid group of plants, grow widely on Fraser Island, able to support themselves in the sandy soils because their specialised root systems are remarkably efficient at extracting what little phosphorous and other nutriments there are. These mechanisms are not restricted to the plants of the island, they occur in poor soils elsewhere. However Fraser Island's abundance of plants is an indication of how well

Opposite: Smallest of the fruit and nectar-eating bats, the Queensland blossom bat when adult is less than fifty millimetres long. With hook-like 'claws' it clings to flowers like those of the banksias to extract the rich nectar.

Above: Bulges on the trunks of some of the eucalypts are woody tubers storing nutriments so the trees can flourish in the sandy soils of the island.

equipped they are to handle life in the sandy soils and one of the reasons why the island has such a diversity of vegetation.

The flowering trees and shrubs like the banksias, paperbarks, bloodwoods and bottlebrushes of the island with their nectar-rich blossoms are feeding grounds for the tiny Queensland blossom bat, smallest of the herbivorous fruit bats and flying foxes. When fully grown its body is only fifty millimetres long and it weighs about fifteen grams. Its tongue is the same length as its body and projects from a long-pointed muzzle which it dips deep into the flowers. The tongue has minute, brush-like projections for gathering food. The bat has a coat of pale, honey-coloured fur, and hook-like 'claws' on its wings help it cling to the flower stalks as it feeds. It feeds at night, sheltering during the day in the dense foliage of the forest and, like others of the fruit and nectar-eating bats it does not hibernate. By concentrating on the nectar the blossom bat is restricted to forests where some flowers are in bloom all year round. In the tropics and places like Fraser Island the bat, whose territory covers the coastal strip from near the New South Wales border to the tip of Cape York, is an import-

ant pollinator. The blossom bat, although so small, can be aggressive when it is hovering to feed. It will flap its wingtips together and attack others approaching the nectar-filled flowers.

Fraser Island is also part of the habitat of the grey-headed flying fox, a much larger creature whose diet includes native fruits as well as the nectar of eucalypt blossoms. The bats congregate on the island in September in groups of 30 000 or so and their behaviour follows a clear social order. Old males form a guard around the group; inside the colony are the harem females. From September to October their young are born to be left in a crèche while the mothers go out at night to feed. They return to their own babies in the midst of the huge group. The bats leave the island in May when the weather gets colder and food becomes scarce.

The first major study of Fraser Island's mammals, reptiles and frogs, made in 1962, and subsequent studies of the last few years (and which are continuing) have revealed that although there is a wide diversity there are few specific numbers, due, it is concluded, to the generally low food supplies in the sandy environment. The largest number of any species occurs where the richest food supplies are found. Twenty or so land mammals, five marine mammals, twenty amphibians and forty-six land reptiles have been identified on Fraser Island. There are fewer frogs on the island than on North Stradbroke, the neighbouring island which is only one fifth the size of Fraser Island. The reason is that amphibians need land to spread and they were able to work their way across the land bridge once linking North and South Stradbroke Islands with the mainland.

Like most of the island's plants the animals of Fraser Island are found elsewhere and most occur in the similar environment of the neighbouring islands and parts of the Cooloola sandmass. Some probably floated across the strait dividing Fraser Island from the mainland on rafts of logs in times of flood but some strange, unexplained questions remain unanswered: why, for example, are there no koalas on Fraser Island when they occur on North Stradbroke?

Fraser Island's isolation may be one reason for the survival of the dingoes there. There are none on North Stradbroke Island although they have been seen on Bribie Island. Naturalists investigating these intriguing puzzles assume they were exterminated by early settlers and farmers on North Stradbroke Island in the 1800s.

The bobuck, or mountain possum, a relative of the brushtail possum, occurs on Fraser Island although no brushtails or ringtails have been recorded there. The bobuck was once more abundant than today but it fell victim to the guns of the early timber-getters after it became a pest around the camp at Central Station. It spends most of its time in the trees but comes down to the ground to feed on shrubs, fruits, buds, fungi and lichen and there it is prey to the dingo and python. If alarmed the bobuck will take to the water; perhaps it swam across Great Sandy Strait to Fraser Island. In 1973 a lone eastern grey kangaroo, assumed to have swum across the channel, put in a brief appearance at the forestry station at Ungowa on the west coast, opposite the narrowest point of the strait.

Swamp wallabies, about one metre high, have also been found on the island. They differ from their mainland relations by being more thickset and having a golden coloured pelt instead of the more common brownish to black. Fraser and North Stradbroke Islands are the

Above: Cane toads are usurping the habitat of many of Fraser Island's native creatures. They breed prolifically in lagoons and swamps behind the coastal foredunes.

Below: Silken webs of the orb-weaving spiders lace the undergrowth.

only sand islands where these creatures have been recorded. The most common mammal on Fraser Island is the southern bush rat. It inhabits the rainforest, open forest, low woodland and foredunes. The feathertail glider, squirrel glider and carnivorous marsupial and bush and water rats all have been collected on the island.

Fraser Island is also the only sand island where the nocturnal yellow-footed *Antechinus* has been collected. This small, carnivorous, mouse-like creature is colourful both in appearance and habit. It is well known to many house-holders in its

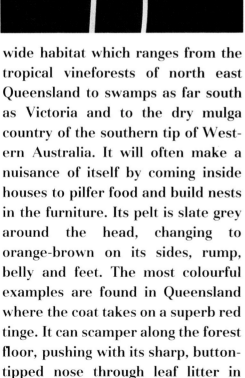

Left: Throughout the year the undergrowth is studded with delicate orchids like the flying duck orchid.

Right: Phaius australis, big, bold and beautiful, Australia's largest-flowering native orchid, bursts into extravagant bloom in late winter.

wide habitat which ranges from the tropical vineforests of north east Queensland to swamps as far south as Victoria and to the dry mulga country of the southern tip of Western Australia. It will often make a nuisance of itself by coming inside houses to pilfer food and build nests in the furniture. Its pelt is slate grey around the head, changing to orange-brown on its sides, rump, belly and feet. The most colourful examples are found in Queensland where the coat takes on a superb red tinge. It can scamper along the forest floor, pushing with its sharp, button-tipped nose through leaf litter in search of insects or small birds. Shortly after mating the males die, leaving the pregnant females to give birth to their young in an environment free of competition. The most common rodent of the sedge swamps is the grassland melomys.

The dingoes and the brumbies are the most noticeable of the introduced animals on Fraser Island. A few of the residents keep cats and some of these have escaped into the bush to breed. But the animal which seems to be gaining a real hold is the cane toad. It has invaded parts of the island and has settled in large numbers along the east coast where it breeds in the brackish water of lagoons behind the foredunes. A native of south and central America, the cane toad was introduced to north Queensland in 1935 to control a beetle pest which plagued sugar cane plantations. The venture was not a success; the toad liked its new home and spread rapidly so that today it is distributed from Cape York to north eastern NSW. The only place to escape invasion in the Great Sandy Region is Moreton Island. The toad competes with the local fauna for resting places, food and breeding sites. It preys heavily on native animals such as small snakes, lizards and frogs and toxins secreted from glands along its back poison creatures when they try to eat it.

The forests are the realm of the orchids, a fantasy of flowers embroidering the undergrowth from tiny pale green-hoods to delicate pinks, creams and rich purple blooms at different times of the year. Orchid Beach gets its name from the hyacinth orchid which sends up its spikes of dark pink mottled blooms from amongst the leaf mould of the eucalypts.

Of the many orchids on Fraser Island, the big, bold *Phaius australis* is probably the most spectacular. It has no common name. It grows tall and proud – up to two metres high – among the shrubs of the open canopy and its flowers, creamy rich on the edges deepening to a lush brown-red in the centre are reminiscent of old brocade. They are the largest of any of Australia's native orchids. The *Phaius australis* bursts into its extravagant bloom in late winter. The orchid also grows on the other sand islands and until recently, was prolific in parts of the coastal mainland. It also thrives on some of the islands of the Pacific Ocean.

The undergrowth shelters a host of insects and spiders. The wolf spider, common throughout Australia, lives on the ground in the island's dry country, in the swamps and along the beach strands. Often mistaken for a trapdoor from its habit of making a rough trapdoor for its burrow, the wolf spider has a row of four very small eyes in front of two rows each with two large eyes. The female is a devoted mother; she carries the egg sac attached to her web-spinning organ until the young hatch. They remain, clustered over her body and legs so that she resembles a ball of fluff, until they are old enough to fend for themselves.

The beautiful silken webs of the golden orb weaver are found on

Fraser Island close to the ground or suspended about ten metres up in the trees. Another spider widespread in Australia, the golden orb is interesting because of the huge difference in size between male and female, the most marked of any of Australia's spiders. The male seems puny beside his robust mate. Another orb weaver, the large-jawed spider, builds its web in the island's swamps and across narrow streams. The male is a superb master of disguise; he folds his legs into pairs, hiding them along twigs or reeds. When disturbed the large-jawed spider will drop to the water below and skate across its surface to safety.

Jumping spiders are also part of the world of miniature creatures on the island. The female goes through several moults before she is mature, protecting herself in a silken chamber she weaves around herself. Towards the end of the final moult she is sexually attractive and is approached by a male spider which catches her attention by special signals and which repulses intruders if they come too close. Both spiders are about the same size and this enables the male to escape after mating. He puts her into a kind of trance long enough for his getaway, unlike some other species where the female kills the male after mating.

GIANTS WITH THEIR FEET IN THE SAND

GIANTS WITH THEIR FEET IN THE SAND

The king of the commercial forests is the blackbutt tree, logged on Fraser Island and used in replanting programs by the forestry department. It is distinguished by its dark, stringy base and pale trunk and branches, a forest giant often growing thirty metres high. In 1926 trees with a diameter of two metres and with their first limbs twenty metres above the ground were logged. One of Australia's 600-odd species of indigenous eucalypts, blackbutt grows on the tops of ridges in well-drained localities surrounding the rainforests. Its timber is extremely hard and strong; it was used for the load-bearing supports of buildings up to six storeys high in the early days and is still in demand as a building timber for houses, bridges and posts and telephone poles.

Also growing in the high central dunes is tallow wood, another eucalyptus. It has rough, closely woven bark and broad leaves. A large, spreading tree, it is now rare and only selectively logged. Records from the first two decades of the century reported tallow woods with a diameter of more than two metres and a height of twenty-four metres from the ground to the first limbs. It has been used for house stumps and frames, poles and posts and even for flooring in dance halls.

Another eucalypt of the high dunes is red bloodwood with irregular-patterned bark. In summer, when bloodwoods put on their spectacular display of heavily-scented flowers, they are alive during the day with squabbling lorikeets and at night with fruit and nectar-eating bats. Scattered in the forest among the scribbly gums are yet other eucalypts, forest red gums, ironbarks and Moreton Bay ash. Forest red gums grow up to twenty metres in height and have a smooth, grey-pink

Previous page: Nature creates patterns with ferns in the rainforest depths.

bark; Moreton Bay ash have a smooth grey trunk, coated around the base with rough, tesselated bark. Some other smaller trees growing in the high open forests are sheoaks, wattles, banksias and coastal cypress pines, the cone-shaped 'Christmas trees' with dark, grooved straight stems and fern-like foliage. The bushland is a mosaic of textures and colours, an enchanted wood and, amazingly, all growing on sand.

Among the plants of the forest floor are bush iris with purple flowers appearing from late August to October, slender rice flower with clusters of either white or pink flowers in winter and spring, wedding bush which is transformed from a dark green shrub into a mass of white flowers in spring and boronias, of which there are several varieties on the island so that flowers can be found in most months of the year.

One of the interesting smaller trees thriving in the sheltered high dunes is the blueberry ash, or olive berry, its name derived from the small berries which follow the bell-shaped creamy flower clusters. The flowers appear in summer and have a slight aroma of aniseed. The berries stay on the trees for most of autumn and winter and are eagerly sought by birds.

Another tree sought by the timber industry is the brush box or *tristania*. A lofty giant, it may grow to forty metres and has a reddish trunk and branches. Brush box adapts well to dry conditions and is familiar as a street tree in many Australian cities where it is regularly lopped to contain its spreading shape. Clusters of white flowers appear in summer.

Hardwoods form the bulk of commercial timber taken from Fraser Island's forest today with blackbutt and brush box making up the largest volume followed by *satinay* and small quantities of red mahogany, a eucalypt which is used for flooring and weatherboards.

The *satinay's* common name, turpentine, comes from the reddish-brown resin it exudes and which gives the tree its most valuable commercial attribute – resistance to shipworms and termites. Consequently its tall straight stems have been in great demand for wharf piles and boatbuilding. Turpentines from Fraser Island were used for extensions to London's Tilbury Docks in 1928-29 and for sidings in the Suez Canal during World War Two. It was first harvested in 1915 when trees measuring two point five metres in diameter at breast height were recorded. At Pile Valley, near Cent-

Soaring to the sky, a rainforest giant stretches its crown to the sun.

Left: Fragile tongue orchids make their home clinging to the trunk of a hoop pine.

Right: The distinctive trunk of Moreton Bay ash. Around its base it wears a chequered covering of tesselated bark and, above, a smooth coat which varies from grey to blue-green with the seasons.

ral Station in the heart of the rainforest, there is a magnificent stand of turpentines. Queensland's colonial botanist, Walter Hill, who visited Fraser Island during his term of office between 1859 and 1881, gave his name to the island's turpentine, *Syncarpia hillii*. It was called peebeen by the Aborigines.

Among the turpentine's neighbours in the island's rainforest are the towering kauri pines, uncommon in other Queensland rainforests. They are not true pines as they have a broad green sickle-shaped leaf instead of needles. Slow growing, they belong to an ancient family

which gets its name from the Greek word meaning a ball of string, a reference to the large fruit or cones they bear. Kauri pines have tall, straight stems, often mottled with pink, grey-green and creamy blotches, a patchwork of colours worked by nature in the rainforest damp. The kauris were the first of the island's trees to be harvested and milled at Maryborough in the 1860s. They were given the Aboriginal name of the tree, Dundathu.

He was stationed there from 1913 until 1920 and later became deputy forester for Queensland. The kauri is rich in long-lasting resin which often survives longer than the trees themselves and, in its fossilised form, is known as copal and used commercially in the production of some kinds of varnish. The timber found its way into shelving, flooring and lining and was useful for joinery, cabinet-making and plywood.

Like the kauri, the hoop pine is another indigenous softwood, a member of the family to which monkey puzzle trees, bunya and Norfolk Island pines, all conifers of the southern hemisphere, belong. On Fraser Island hoop pines grow naturally in small patches in the centre of the island. They are cone-shaped with smooth boles and thick tufts of needle-like foliage. There are still a few rare specimens of white beech growing on Fraser Island. Early this century huge veterans more than twenty-five metres tall and two metres in diameter were logged for their highly-prized timber to be used for decking, small craft and wood carving. A native of coastal rainforest, the white beech is now scarce and no longer logged. At Central Station there is a magnificent stand of spotted gums, tall straight trees the trunks of which are covered with smooth grey and cream mottled bark, and a copse of flooded gums planted in 1950.

Beneath the protective canopy provided by the rainforest giants, tangled vines thread themselves into a mesh of loops through palms and ferns and, on the forest floor, a diminutive woodland of lichens and mosses, fungus and orchids grows - lilliputians among the leviathans. In his novel, *The Eye of the Storm,* Patrick White described the rainforest ...'the trees were so densely massed, the columns so mass upholstered or lichen encrusted, the vines suspended from them so intricately rigged, the light barely slithered down ...'

The big trees are life-givers to the smaller plants of the rainforest which is about five per cent of the island's sandmass and which grows on the dunes of system four, the apex of the island's botanical attainment. Most of the nutriments of the rainforest are waving around in the breeze, leaves waiting to fall to form a lush mat on the ground, and strands of fungus, the hyphae, abounding in the moist layers of leaf litter where they are associated with the decaying matter.

Two of Australia's largest cockroaches churn through the leaf mulch of the island's rainforest floor. Some of the biggest in the world, they grow to eight centimetres long and are a handsome burnished brown colour. Wingless, they build spiral burrows about five centimetres deep in the sand at the end of which they store dead leaves. When the leaves are broken down by bacteria the cockroaches are able to digest the mouldy mass. Unlike many of Australia's 400-odd species of cockroach, these of south east Queensland's rainforests give birth to live young. Several other kinds of cockroach have been found on the island from among the leaf litter, under dead bark and in fallen logs. Their close relatives, termites, have also been studied in the Great Sandy Region. Twenty species, including two which appear to be new to science, were identified. Being wood eaters they were found on all dune systems with some restricted to particular areas.

Earthworms are also significant in the story of soil formation and they help to turn over the sands. One hundred years ago Charles Darwin published figures on the rates at which earthworms can move soil. By studying worm casts, scientists in western Europe have estimated that from about 500 to more than 9000 grams per square metre of soil can be turned over in a year by one worm. In Africa the figures are even greater: more than 10000 grams per square metre. Until 1976 only two species of earthworm had been recorded on the dunes of south east Queensland, then, in the last few years, a study identified eighteen more, two of which so far appear to be only on Fraser Island and new to science. The scientist investigating the earthworms has suggested that the creature may have developed genetic differences because of enforced isolation in the moist, humid pockets it needs to survive. The sand environment is usually too dry for the worms and they bury deep under the surface to congregate in small patches – around trees and in swamps – where there are concentrations of organic material.

Genetic differences were observed in dry areas where separated colonies were found. Other earthworms are common throughout the damp rainforest. The largest earthworms found measured eighty centimetres. As with many of the island's life forms questions remain unanswered about these creatures. Their reproductive habits are still not fully understood and their lifespan is a questionmark. Their diversity on Fraser Island matches the diversity and progress of vegetation across the dunes. They appear to

Above: The rainforest giants nurture smaller plants: ferns, mosses, fungus and lichens cluster in the shelter provided by the tall trees.

Below: Survivor from past ages, the king fern Angiopteris is a remnant of the steamy jungles of 250 million years ago and has fronds up to five metres long.

introduce an organic mat to their burrows to be acted on by fungi and bacteria and some earthworms have enzymes able to break down cellulose, the substance constituting the cell walls of plants, in wood. Others, like the giant cockroaches, have fallen leaves in their burrows where bacteria help speed up the cycle.

Rotting logs on the damp forest floor are both food and shelter for the giant rainforest snail. It ventures out at night to feed almost exclusively on decaying timber, returning to the protection of the logs during the daytime. It is rarely seen in daytime and only when the forest is misty with light rain. One of several snails of the rainforest, the giant snail is sometimes called the apple snail because of its round shape. Apple snails have been found as big as a man's fist and are a rich, glossy brown. They live a long time, taking about five years to reach maturity, and are hermaphrodites, that is, each animal has both male and female organs of reproduction. Specimens have been collected carrying up to fifty eggs. Bushfires claim many victims, and reptiles and rats take them. The Aborigines used their tough shells as scrapers.

In 1976 a bizarre, subterranean creature new to science was discovered by accident in the sands of Cooloola and Fraser Island. The only addition this century to the 2000-strong Australian members of the cricket family, it became known as the Cooloola Monster. The first specimen, about five centimetres long, dropped into a trapping container sunk by spider specialists from the Queensland Museum on a collecting survey of Cooloola's rainforest in February of that year. With other non-spider specimens it was bottled away for almost a year until the museum's entomologists, during a routine sorting, realised it was an exciting find.

The hunt was on to find more specimens. The scientists laid baits of oatmeal in the mistaken belief that, like other crickets, the monster would find them irresistible.

The monster is, in fact, carnivorous, its diet mainly the larvae of the scarab beetle. A public appeal brought to light two small specimens, one from a fisherman's tent at Cooloola and one dug from building foundations on Fraser Island. The search was on in earnest. Special gutter traps used overseas were made by the CSIRO in Canberra and shipped to Queensland. The scientists caught lots of creatures but no

The Cooloola Monster, a creature belonging to the cricket family, was discovered in 1976. The female, pale, wingless and with tiny eyes and large digging spurs, spends her life underground.

monsters. Two expeditions were made in 1978 to capture the elusive female which so far had failed to make an appearance. The traps were unsuccessful. Then, more specimens were found on Fraser Island – a male near the *Maheno* wreck one hundred metres above the beach, and a female, immobilised by an ant lion near Sandy Cape Lighthouse. She was forced out by heavy rain. The crew filming *Sands of Time* found a male during the shoot at the Queensland National Park and Wildlife Service camp at Dundabara.

The Cooloola Monster has adapted to life underground and the female lives entirely underground. She struggles back to the protection of the sand if she is disturbed or forced out by very wet weather. Her eyes have degenerated into mere dots. She is larger and paler than her mate, totally wingless, the abdomen is grossly inflated and her legs are shorter and stouter than those of other crickets and bear remarkable flattened digging spurs. The male has developed a bit of a suntan – he is pale brown – to cope with his infrequent sorties above ground to find a mate, and he is slimmer and his hind legs are longer than the female's. Antennae of both male and female are reduced to suit their sub-terranean habits. The entomologists have suggested that the monster is widespread throughout the Great Sandy Region and is not confined to rainforest. They conclude the extraordinary animal is one of the unique features of the region and say its discovery is an entomological event of world-wide significance, confirming the evolutionary antiquity of the sand-adapted animal and plant life of the island and its neighbouring coastal sand mass.

Woolgoobver Creek runs through the rainforest at Central Station. It winds down to the west coast and one of the tram tracks used in the older timber days followed its course to the sea. The name of the creek refers to the Aborigines' name for the macrozamia palm, the primitive plant halfway between a fern and a palm whose bright orange fruit they used for a kind of mash. Crystal clear waters of the stream flow over a pure white sandy bed, in some places tinged a pale jade green with algae, in some places a latticework of shadows as ferns dip their fronds into the water. Some splendid palms and ferns grow along its banks in the cool green tent of the rainforest. Occasionally a dingo comes down to drink and the sunlight filters through the umbrella of the forest canopy.

The wonderful, rare *Angiopteris* fern, appropriately named king fern, grows four metres tall and its fronds reach up to five metres long. It is amongst the largest in the world and has been described as a living fossil. It evolved in the earth's steamy jungles 250 million years ago and it has not changed genetically since then. Once it grew almost like a weed in the tropical areas of the globe but today it is very scarce, having retreated to refuges like some isolated islands. Carnarvon Gorge in central Queensland and Fraser Island, which has several magnificent, flourishing king ferns, are the only places where it grows outside the tropics. Other tree ferns adorn the forest. The Aborigines used the fronds of some tree ferns, roasted, as medicines. Vines looping through the trees include climbing pandanus, wild passion flower and hoya, the plant which produces bunches of sweet scented small velvety flowers looking remarkably like the hand-made floral decorations women once used to smarten up their straw hats. A spongey mattress of mosses, lichens and fungi covers parts of the forest floor. Sphagnum moss, known to gardeners as the peat moss for potting mixtures, reaches the northern limit of its range on the island and is found in small patches.

The large trees are often hosts to other plants: spores of ferns and mosses drift through the air and become lodged on the branches and trunks of the forest giants; other plants – staghorns, elkhorns and orchids – collect their moisture from the air and their nutriments from leaf mould on the trees. Brush box trees are popular hosts for strangler figs in the island's rainforests where they clasp the trunks forming huge, winged buttresses. The fig seeds often germinate in crevices in the limbs of trees and their roots reach down to the ground. They wrap themselves around their hosts and after long decades their own crown of leaves can stifle the host's supply of light and it will die. The figs take over as self supporting hollow, twisted columns.

An old tree that dies and falls is the chance many other plants are waiting for. Not only does a fallen forest giant provide food for many of the creatures of the forest floor, but the gap it leaves in the canopy ceiling allows small saplings to grow up to the patch of light it reveals, and sunlight, admitted to the ground, enables seeds that may have lain dormant for years to sprout. The forest is continually regenerating.

WHERE THE SANDS RUN OUT

WHERE THE SANDS RUN OUT

The west coast of Fraser Island is the end of the long journey for the sands of time. In trickles and wisps they slip down the face of the old, weathered dunes to the mosaic of mudflats bordering the shoreline. This is the tidal zone: estuaries and inlets washed twice daily by the sea, a strand of sheltered waters, sea grasses and mangrove swamps.

Two great scoops form the shoreline of the west coast, separated from the mainland by the shallow waters of Great Sandy Strait. The strait is dotted with several small islands, two of which, Woody and Little Woody, are national parks. Under the silty bed of the strait are the remains of old trees, once tall forests growing high on the dunes, now overtaken by the relentless sands. Aborigines used to wade across the strait and paddle over it in their bark canoes.

The mudflats and sandbanks have built up as a result of the outflow of the Mary River which has a large catchment area and heavy runoff and brings silt from the mainland to meet the sea. Its outflow is carried by the tides that funnel through Hervey Bay. The tidal wetlands are constantly replenished by new supplies of silt from the mainland and creeks and streams entering the sea from the island.

The shimmering heat haze hanging over the brackish water and shallow flats, the sticky squelch of mud, the pervasive odour of ooze and the myriad small biting insects are enough to deter most beach lovers, but the island's western shoreline is second only to the rainforests as a fertile source of life. The languid waters and currents that stir the sea bottom and the fresh water fed by the streams help spread rotting debris and it is a rich feeding ground for a wide variety of sea creatures. The abundant sea grasses and mangroves nurture the entire food chain, from drifting marine organisms too small to see with the naked eye to worms, crabs, fish and sharks. The entire area of the strait has been described as equal to or better than the best farmlands for productivity.

Previous page: Journey's end for the sands – the west coast where the dunes meet the placid waters of Great Sandy Strait.

Huge swathes of tidal seagrasses are maritime pastures for the sea-cow or dugong, the only existing herbivorous mammal in the world living exclusively in the sea. The waters of the Great Sandy Strait and Hervey Bay are thought to shelter some of the largest numbers of these creatures in the world. Dugongs are also found in parts of the east coast of Africa, south Asia, the New Hebrides and New Caledonia. Its relatives are the manatees which are found in both sea and freshwater in parts of the Caribbean and Atlantic. Today the dugong is a vulnerable species and seldom seen. Like the dolphins and sea turtles the dugongs are threatened by extension of a shark trawling program in Hervey and Wide Bays.

Dugongs may grow to between two and three metres in length and weigh on average 400 kilograms, the huge mass helping them to stay submerged while they graze. They have short, mobile snouts. The male has small, ivory tusks and the female mammary glands and teats. She clasps her baby with her flippers as it suckles, a characteristic which may have prompted mariners of old to give the dugongs the name of mermaids. Dugongs' thick rubbery hides are often scarred from encounters with boats or jagged coral reefs. They were hunted for their oil, said to aid treatment of rheumatic and lung disorders, for their hides, used as leather, and their bones, which yielded a particularly good charcoal for sugar refining.

During the 1930s thousands of dugongs were netted and slaughtered for their oil in the sea grass meadows off Bogimbah on the island's west coast. A female yielded about fifty-eight litres and the males from eighteen to twenty-two litres. The fishermen received about four pounds per four litres for oil.

The Aborigines of Fraser Island had a crafty method of capturing the gentle giants. They used a spear with a specially weakened shaft. As the speared animal twisted and turned the shaft broke, leaving one piece embedded in its flesh. The hunter retrieved the other piece and, returning to camp, did not announce that he had speared a dugong but mentioned where he had found the broken shaft. The injured dugong made for the sanctuary of the nearest creek and next day, at low tide, the men looked for the animal along the estuary of the creek. The Aborigines were very adept at cutting up the flesh.

Fraser Island's waters also har-

The tidal shores of Fraser Island shelter several kinds of mangrove which have different ways of propagation.

Above left: The cannon ball mangrove produces a seed pod.

Above right: The large-leaved mangrove (known to the Aborigines as Kowinaka or Birree) and, below, the small-stilted mangrove produce live young. The seedlings drop to the mud where they take root.

boured another large creature – a strange sea monster described as being halfway between a crocodile and a turtle. Occasional sightings of sea monsters near the island have been reported until recently by fishermen so it is possible that a mysterious denizen of the deep is lurking somewhere around Sandy Cape. The Aborigines called it Moha Moha and told stories of how it had attacked their camps, that it had legs and fingers and was good to eat.

Joseph Banks, on Cook's expedition of 1770 in the *Endeavour*, recorded sighting a huge sea creature off Sandy Cape: 'A grampus of

Forerunners of the twisted trees of the mudflats, the young mangroves grow in the protected tidal zone.

Forerunners of the twisted trees of the mudflats, the young mangroves grow in the protected tidal zone.

middle size leaped with his whole body out of the water several times making a splash and foam in the sea as if a mountain had fallen into it.'

Then, 120 years later, in 1891 during her term as schoolteacher at the Sandy Cape Lighthouse village, Shirley Lovell wrote to the Australian Museum in Sydney with her detailed description of a creature, two parts fish and one part turtle, she had watched on the beach at Sandy Cape. She described it as about eleven metres long and its centre section as an enormous dome-shaped carapace over two metres high.

'It lay stretched on the shore with

its huge mouth agape and the glossy skin of its head, neck and fish-like tail gleaming in the sun' she wrote. She observed the creature for half an hour, making sketches of it, until suddenly, giving its tail a half twist, 'it shot off like a flash of lightning and I saw its tail about a quarter of a mile off'.

Miss Lovell also reported another large creature, known to the Aborigines as womang, which fitted later biologists' descriptions of a manta ray. Her reports were not taken seriously and she was lampooned by having the creature named after her in a facetious account published in 1893 in *The Great Barrier Reef of Australia: Its Products and Potentialities* by W Sackville Kent. A fishing party on the island in 1964 found a sea monster, its flesh badly decomposed and partly eaten by dingoes and eagles; the description and drawing the party made of it bore a close resemblance to the creature reported by Miss Lovell.

The mangroves, trees whose roots have extraordinary ways of getting their oxygen supplies in the fine, sticky mud, shelter and provide for a host of marine creatures. There are at least eight kinds of mangrove growing in the tidal mudflats off the island. Some have aerial prop roots which branch out and help anchor the plant in the soft mud. The red mangrove, a favoured haunt of the mud crab, develops aerial roots on the stem. Reaching higher and higher they form a spreading tangle abutting the tree several metres from mud level. Others, like the grey mangrove, have roots which run horizontally in the mud and put up spikes which act as breathing tubes. Still others, such as the large fruited orange mangrove and the black mangrove, put out roots which curve through the mud like writhing serpents. Near the tops of the exposed curves they develop additional knobby roots to help the plants breathe. Many mangroves produce live young; the cigar-shaped seedlings grow out of the flowers, dropping to the mud to take root.

The milky mangrove is called 'blind your eyes' because its milky sap is bitterly pungent and causes a painful burning sensation in the throat, headache and even temporary blindness if it gets in the eyes. Its sap was used as a substitute for rubber to mend rubber goods and its white wood was thinly sliced and woven into baskets. Another curious tree of the intertidal zone is the swamp oak which grows with its feet in the wet. The Great Sandy Strait and neighbouring estuaries are the only places it does so.

As the tide falls on the mudflats fiddler crabs appear at the tops of their burrows, suspicious and ready to dart back to safety if danger threatens. Male fiddler crabs have an enlarged, bright yellow claw, sometimes as big as their bodies. The crab brandishes the claw – either the right or the left – while sifting food from the mud with the other, rather like a diner shielding his mouth with one hand while he picks his teeth with the other.

Several parts of the waterways adjacent to the island have been set aside as fisheries habitat reserves including the strip of Great Sandy Strait near the Mary River Heads to the Fraser Island shoreline. Its fairly undisturbed state makes the area one of Queensland's most interesting marine environments.

By 1900 fishing was well established in the waters around the island and commercial fishing there today accounts for almost one quarter of the total of finned fish and up to one third of the total of mud crabs landed in Queensland. Prawn trawlers work in Hervey Bay although the best prawning waters are off the east coast. Restrictions cover commercial

as well as recreational fishing and control such things as the kind and length (but not the number) of the catch and the sort of equipment to be used to protect the marine resources of these waters.

Commercial fishermen have developed a method known as 'tunnelling off' which overcomes the problems of using conventional seine nets on the mudflats and takes advantage of the habits of some kinds of fish which gather around shallow underwater banks at high tide. Two fishermen, in dinghies, stake a net around the banks and as the tide falls the fish are collected in the part of the net known as the tunnel. Sea mullet congregate in the shoals of bays and estuaries and migrate miles up the coast to spawn. The young return south to the feeding grounds. Whiting, fine-boned and delicious to eat, make up the bulk of the finned fish harvested in the Fraser Island region, with tailor, bream, mackerel and flathead among the remainder. Fishing is a year round activity with the peak of the prawn and mullet catches in April and whiting and tailor from August to September.

Great Sandy Strait has two small coral reefs, a total of about thirty-five hectares. They are off the shore

Brandishing its enlarged yellow claw to ward off intruders, a fiddler crab stands guard at the entrance to its burrow.

Opposite: The places where creeks enter the sea along the island's western beaches are good feeding grounds for wading birds like the royal spoonbill.

between Woody and Round Islands and contain about forty different kinds of hard and soft corals. In the ocean, offshore from Sandy Cape and Waddy Point, are two other coral reefs. An artificial reef, one of the largest in Australia, was built from old motor car bodies and tyres in the underwater basin separating the two indentations in Fraser Island's western shore. It has provided a fish breeding ground and resulted in an increase in the numbers and kinds of fish, including some reef fish not previously recorded in the region.

The island's western beaches are strewn with relics of its past. They are the graveyards of ancient forests which flourished hundreds of thousands of years ago. Trees were buried by the drifting sands and then exhumed as the sands moved. Present sea levels are the highest for 30 000 years. In past ages dunes supporting thick forests flourished where the shoreline is now and also across the strait. As the sands drove onward and the seas rose, trees were submerged, first by sand and gradually by the sea. Remains of those ancient forests lie as gnarled lumps of weather-worn sand rock or as beds of peat. Protruding here and

there from the peat are blackened banksia seed cones. Truncated stems of turpentine trees, forlorn vestiges of forest giants, emerge like suspended fossils through the white sand of the beach. Their stems were preserved deep in the dunes once covering this part of the island. Salt, sand, wind and rain have sawn them off just above the surface and they will gradually continue to fret away until, in a few hundred years, nothing is left. Their presence on the beach is a sign that other remnants of former plant colonies lie under the silt of Great Sandy Strait.

The sight of huge birds of prey soaring over the island's shores is awe inspiring, uplifting to the spirit and a realisation that nature's balance can still be maintained on the fragile island of sand if it is protected from exploitation and improper use. Eagles, kites, hawks and the superb osprey make the entire island their domain. The handsome brahminy kite, common on Australia's northern coasts, is a distinctive *habitué* of the island's mangrove swamps with its chestnut coloured back and white head and chest. In the mangrove swamps there is plenty of food to satisfy its diet of crabs, fish, small reptiles and the flotsam of the sea. Its nest, sometimes bedecked with ribbons of seaweed, is built of sticks, often in the tops of mangrove trees.

The brahminy kite is joined in the tidal inlets by the whistling kite, named for its shrill call. It is a scavenger, living on the carrion deposited by the tides. Occasionally a pair can be seen swooping in the air currents over the island, keeping a sharp lookout for dead creatures on the ground. The rare square-tailed kite frequents the island for the good pickings along beaches and the black-shouldered kite, a smaller, more delicate bird, is distinguished by a small black patch under its wings, seen as the bird makes its direct, gull-like flights.

Small birds are the usual prey of the brown goshawk and its close relatives, the collared sparrowhawk and grey goshawk, all birds widely distributed throughout Australia. The grey goshawk is a beautiful bird, either pearly grey or white, which chases small birds. Like other goshawks the female is much bigger than the male. Females have been trained for falconry. Peregrine falcons, once common throughout Australia but declining in numbers as their habitats are overtaken by settlement, hunt in pairs around the island's coasts. Very fast flyers, they circle their prey and dive at high speed, striking their victims on the head with their hind claws or fastening onto the prey in mid air. Other falcons and the nankeen kestrel, which is usually rare on Queensland's coasts, have been sighted on Fraser Island.

Gracefully scooping up its prey from the sea with its long-curved talons, the osprey is a thoroughly efficient hunter and the waters of Great Sandy Strait provide plenty of game. It hovers over the sea then plunges feet first to grasp its prey by the head. It flies to a high branch to enjoy its meal, its victim a silver flash to the onlooker. On Fraser Island ospreys build their enormous nests of twigs close to their hunting grounds and line them with seaweed. They use these nests year after year, adding to the structure each season. Other raptors of the island's shores are the sea eagle, often seen hunting in pairs as it hovers low over the water before dropping to snatch up its prey, and the wedge tailed eagle, or eaglehawk, the huge dark bird with a wingspan of up to two and a half metres. It sails majestically over the island from coast to coast, monitoring activity on the dunes below.

Waterfowl of the inshore waters include Australia's largest flying bird, the pelican, and its relative, the Australian gannet, and several kinds of duck and cormorant which fish the estuaries. Wading birds such as egrets, ibis, herons and spoonbills stalk gracefully through the mudflats in search of food. The black swan, Australia's only native swan, congregates in large numbers in the strait. Flocks of the birds sail with stately dignity over the brackish waters, their long necks arched in elegant curves as they dip their heads to feed. When disturbed the birds take off in successive waves, churning the waters as they rise to wend their way across the sky, their sad trumpeting and honking echoing over the sea.

THE GIANT SPONGE

THE GIANT SPONGE

Sand and water dominate the Fraser Island story – millions of tonnes of sand frequently washed by storms and rain, an average of 1500 millimetres each year. The giant sandcastle is an enormous sponge absorbing water, using some of it to recycle plants and dissolve minerals for its soils and some to feed its creeks, streams and lakes. Some of it cuts gullies and channels through the dunes but most of it is stored in a vast underground reservoir. The links between the sand and the water are ageless, as old as the island itself, and their relationship is endless.

Fraser Island and its neighbouring coastal sand mass lie in a subtropical zone between weather systems bringing cool season rains to southern Australia and strong, dominant summer rains to the tropical north. The Great Sandy Region receives both summer and winter rains and it is never fiercely hot or very cold. It escaped the worst of the violent winds and periods of dryness of the last of the Great Ice Ages because the colder temperatures of those times forced the southern winter rains north and compensated for reduced summer rains.

Fraser Island's wettest months are in late summer, January to March,

the driest during late winter to spring, August and September. January is usually the hottest month – its maximum temperatures range from about twenty to twenty seven degrees Celsius – and July is the coldest with temperatures ranging from about thirteen to nineteen degrees Celsius. In contrast to the southern parts of the continent where most rains fall during the winter, the island's heaviest falls coincide with the longest days and produce the plants' most active growing time.

Most of the water falling as rain soaks through the sand which, when saturated, can hold up to thirty per cent of its volume of water. The

Previous page: Sand and water, secrets of life on Fraser Island.

upper limit of the saturated sand is the water table and on Fraser Island it follows a line shown on a cross section diagram of the dunes as a gradual, even curve starting at sea level and rising to its highest point in the centre of the island. The underground water has been described as a lens in the sand; the lakes and swamps are the top edge of the lens. Constantly replenished by rain the water remains in the sand for an incredibly long time – up to sixty years – slowly sinking deeper and deeper until it meets the water table where it seeps out in rivulets near the coast. The flow is constant, little affected by seasonal fluctuations in rainfall because the sandmass releases it at a uniform rate.

Scientists have measured the rate of seepage at Cooloola on the coast and found that the water soaks through the sand at about three fifths of a metre each day. An enormous volume of water is held in Cooloola's dunes, at least nine thousand million cubic metres – enough, it is estimated, to support a town of about 150 000 people. It is considered to be one of the most valuable potential resources of the region for future generations. At Tomago, near Newcastle, underground water from the coastal sands

was first pumped to the surface before World War Two, the plant extracting three million gallons a day.

On Fraser Island the untapped underground water resources are considered to be far greater. From Eli Creek water flows through a rugged gorge of pandanus-lined sandy banks to run fast and clear over the ocean beach to the sea at the rate of five million litres an hour.

Sometimes the water strikes a barrier, a lump of peat or sandrock, and is forced to the surface in bubblers, little rushes of water bursting onto the beach in gouts and springs.

Not all the water falling as rain is immediately mopped up by the huge sponge. Some of it runs over the sand forming channels for creeks and streams to work their way to the sea. There are more than fifty freshwater creeks on Fraser Island running through the dunes. Most enter the sea on the west coast because they have formed in the oldest dunes, those which have endured the effects of weathering for up to almost half a million years. With less vegetation cover than the younger dunes they have been easy prey to water erosion.

Water has also been responsible for sculpturing strange little mineral-

topped pillars of sand in Rainbow Gorge, a valley in the coloured sands behind the beach on the east coast. Only about twelve centimetres high, the pillars form as rain courses through the coloured sand where small patches of hardened minerals dot the surface. The red crusts of minerals, impervious to water, protect the impacted white sand beneath them while the surrounding sand is eroded, creating a miniature landscape like a field of red and white toadstools.

Sand is usually porous, highly thirsty stuff. Tip a cup of water onto it during a beach picnic and it rapidly

sinks into the ground. It comes as a surprise to realise some of Fraser Island's sands are non-wetting. They repel water thanks to fungi and the threads of hyphae. When the sands dry out the fungi die, giving the sand a coating impervious to water. The more fungi the greater amount of non-wetting sands.

The younger dunes along the east coast where the vegetation is beginning to establish itself have the greatest amount of non-wetting sands, but they are vulnerable to erosion from what scientists call surface wash. In rainstorms water collects on the non-wetting sands and

Opposite above: Fraser Island's creeks contain some of the purest water in the world.

Below: A landscape of miniature columns and pillars encrusted with minerals has been created by wind and water.

Above: To the Aborigines the laughing waters of the streams were the voice of K'gari, the spirit of Fraser Island.

Below: In a quiet backwater lily pads hide among the reeds.

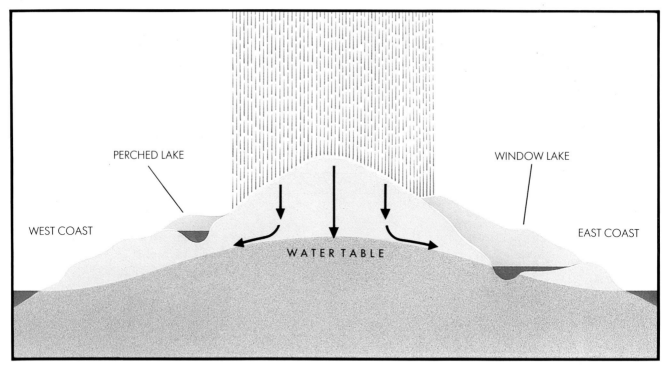

PERCHED LAKE

WINDOW LAKE

WEST COAST

EAST COAST

WATER TABLE

Water falling as rain on the dunes seeps into the sand and emerges when it reaches the water table, the upper limit of the saturated mass of sand, as creeks and streams to flow into the sea.

flows for several metres until soaking into the wettable parts of the dune. To stand on the edge of a sandblow during a rainstorm and see this happening is a remarkable experience – a topsy turvy world where sand and water challenge reason before one's eyes.

Even the fungus cannot withstand the force of heavy rain and the torrential downpours of the cyclones when the sands are slashed by the onslaughts of wind and rain. The harder it rains the more the non-wetting sands erode. Gullies and ditches are gouged out and eaten away as more rain falls.

In the close, thick-wooded forests further inland the picture is different. The sands have fewer fungi to help them and they are porous, but the leafy canopy deflects the rain and litter on the ground acts as a shield against water erosion. However, rain dripping from leaves hits the ground and splashes the sand, flinging the grains aside and paving the way for the destructive effects of water. Try sharing an umbrella and the effect of raindrop splash is apparent. The person holding the umbrella is protected but the other, huddling under the edge of its skirt, collects the rivulets which run down and cascade off the end of the spokes. Surprisingly, the slope of the dunes does not seem to make any difference; water erosion can start from raindrop splash just as quickly on the gently-sloping dunes as on the steep. In the taller forests among the rainforest giants, where the raindrops have a long way to fall, the risk of erosion is increased.

Scientists have sounded a warning bell from their erosion studies on the sands. Because the risk of water erosion is less under the protection of the thick canopy of the close, wooded forests, they caution against any interference that removes the cover. Clearing, burning and vehicle traffic contribute to the increase of erosion. The results of recent studies into the wetting and non-wetting sands have world-wide implications for the regeneration of dunes denuded of plant cover.

A LAKELAND
IN SAND

A LAKELAND IN SAND

Cradled in the dunes of the greatest sand island are more than forty freshwater lakes, bowls of water sitting in sand, some as high as 125 metres above sea level. That water can remain suspended in sand is astonishing but the lakes are not only fascinating places, they are attracting scientific investigation which has led to some interesting conclusions and prompted further speculations about the island's unusual natural history. Fraser Island's lake district is one of very few in Australia, a predominantly arid country. Although lakes occur in dunes in other parts of the world, for example, Nebraska and on King Island in Bass Strait, those in the leached quartz sands of the island may be unique.

Fraser Island's lakes are the highest perched dune lakes in the world. The Boomerang Lakes are 130 metres above sea level and the largest, Lake Boemingen, in the southern part of the island, is 200 hectares in area. More than seventy metres above sea level, it is surrounded by dunes towering a further 120 metres above it. Lake Boemingen was the setting for corroboree scenes for the film, *Eliza Fraser*. The deepest lake is Lake Wabby, eleven metres at its deepest point. The waters of some of the lakes are clear and sparkling with clean, sandy bottoms and beautiful snow white beaches; others have tea-coloured waters, fresh and acidic where life is scarce and much of it primitive and uncommon. The lakes are silent, secluded, deserted sheets of water fringed by forests where time seems to stand still.

Fraser Islanders call the clear waters 'white', the tea-coloured 'black'. Often both may be close together or joined to a single stream. They are an intriguing sight. Lake Jennings is

Previous page: Suspended in sand – Fraser Island has more than forty freshwater lakes cradled in the dunes.

a black lake, connected to Lake Birrabeen, a white lake, by a small channel. The extraordinary phenomenon of black and white waters occurs in other parts of the coastal sand mass and there are black waters in some Canadian lakes while Brazil's Rio Negro was named after the dark colour of its water. Scientists have an explanation for Fraser Island's black and white waters but it remains to be seen whether it is the case for others.

The island's black waters get their colouring from dissolved organic plant material. The white waters come about when water, leaking through the sand, unloads its organic matter on the way and seeps out colourless. Laboratory experiments found that small amounts of iron and aluminium in the sand help remove the organic matter. The clear waters of the creeks and streams which empty to the sea on the ocean coast have been 'bleached' by these mineral coatings on the sand grains as the water passes through them.

There are two kinds of lake in the sand, window and perched. Window lakes are aptly named; they are windows in the water table which form when the ground surface falls below the regional water table and water drains into the depressions. Most window lakes are closer to the coast where the water table is close to the surface and the dunes erode to expose it.

Perched lakes are literally that: the waters sit in a sealed cup in the sand, contained by a membrane of ancient decayed plant material packed hard into a layer of humate. Plant debris collects in hollows in the sand scoured by wind or the folds where dunes meet, and over time settles to form a tough skin impervious to water. In Lake Boemingen ridges of the humate poke through the sand lining the lake floor and are seen as a marbling of dark strands on the pale sand bed. Scientists have suggested that perched lakes may also form in layers of peat found in parts of the embedded coloured sands, bared by the winds scraping depressions in the surface which fill with rainwater. Most perched lakes rely on rain for their water supplies; few are fed by streams.

Lake Bowarrady and its neighbouring lakes in Great Sandy National Park are perched lakes. Bowarrady is high in the dunes, 120 metres above sea level, but is not deep, less than four metres. It is surrounded by paperbark trees and stands of tall hoop pines and other

Above: The tea-coloured
waters of Lake Boemingen,
Fraser Island's largest
perched lake, wash the
milky-white shores.

Below: Submerged leaves
settle in the sparkling
lake water.

Opposite above: A fringe
of encircling trees, reflected
in its calm surface, enfolds
Basin Lake in an
atmosphere of seclusion
and isolation.

Below: Lake McKenzie is an
enchanted place – the
snowy white beaches are
lapped by the crystalline
waters which take on
beautiful colours in
their depths.

rainforest trees, some bearing the
scars where the Aborigines cut bark
for their canoes. Freshwater turtles
pop to the surface of its brown waters, accepting handouts of bread
from visitors.

By contrast, Lake McKenzie, one
of the most beautiful, has crystal
clear rippling waters washing over a
floor of pure white sand deposited
over the impermeable layer by the
wind. Its wide, sheltered beach, protected by the enveloping blackbutt
forest, is sought by holidaymakers.
Lake McKenzie was an important
site for the Aborigines and it is mentioned in DH Lawrence's *Kangaroo*.

Sand spits jut from the shore into the lake like miniature sandblows and may eventually cut it into segments. Following the direction of the south east winds they echo the story of the island's creation.

A small, almost circular lake surrounded by an amphitheatre of wooded hills, Basin Lake has a thin coating of leaves and other organic material on its floor washed down from the eucalypt forests. Clumps of reeds push up through its calm waters exposing the milky-white sand below the fine scum of litter. Concentric rings of dried sedges encircle its banks.

Lake Wabby, a window lake, is flanked on its shoreward side by a massive wall of sand as a sandblow gradually engulfs it. The lake was once much bigger but the blow is slowly swallowing it, and a little companion lake to its south, once part of the same body of water, was cut off by the advancing sand. The lake was fed by an underground stream, now plugged by sand. In the ten years between 1948 and 1958 the dunes advanced more than five metres a year. Today the rate has slowed to about two metres a year but, in time, Lake Wabby will be obliterated.

The sandy shoals at its edge, once rich in rotting plant matter that provides food for several kinds of fish, are being submerged. The waters of Lake Wabby are less acid than most of the other lakes and support nine species of fish, the largest number in any of the lakes. Thirteen different kinds of fish have been identified in the island's lakes and streams. None is unique to Fraser Island although one, a sunfish, is new to science.

The soft-spined rainbow fish, restricted to the freshwater dune lakes and creeks of the coastal sand mass, is the most common fish of Fraser Island's lakes where it thrives because its predator, the mosquito fish, does not occur on the island. Its food includes insects, frogs and tiny freshwater crustaceans. Scientists have so far been unable to explain why two other kinds of fish, normally rarely found together on the mainland, are both in Fraser Island's Ocean Lake. Fish are believed to have been introduced into the island's lakes as eggs on the feet of birds.

Most of the animal life in the lakes is primitive, mainly the aquatic larvae of tiny insects able to survive in the low nutriment levels of the waters. Scientists, using nets, have identified seventy-seven kinds in the sediments of Lake Wabby, more than in any other dune lake in Queensland and northern New South Wales. A primitive member of the tiny midges was found in Lake Boemingen and defied complete identification for several years until 1983 when a scientist in Europe recognized it as related to a creature which had evolved thousands of years ago and is found in the south of Chile. Dragonflies and other tiny flies have been found in the lakes, and also in some streams and bogs. They are part of the food chain for creatures higher up the evolutionary scale.

The quality of the waters in the island's lakes controls the animals living in them and is a reminder of how life on the island has adapted to its unusual environment. Everything grabs every available particle of nutriment from the sandy habitat. Unlike the waters of the sea, the lakes and streams contain very few mineral salts and even these are in low concentrations. Scientists describe the waters as chemically pure. Levels of vegetable plankton are low and they help to make the water acid, both factors inhibiting animal life.

Freshwater molluscs cannot thrive in acid conditions. Light cannot always penetrate acid waters and water plants can only grow in the shallows. Little aquatic life means less food for creatures living around the lakes. Although the scrub is noisy with birdsong there are few waterfowl on the lakes which sit in the dunes hugging their secrets in their depths.

Sometimes the brooding silence is broken by the croaking of frogs. The paperbark swamps and edges of the lakes are the haunt of the acid frogs, creatures at home in the unlikely conditions. Like the giant earthworm which has an acid resistant film on its skin, the frogs have developed a tolerance enabling them to live and breed in the acidic environment.

They are found throughout the coastal sand mass where the high temperatures and humidity suit their breeding habits. The frogs announce their presence with a lot of noise after the rains of late October when they breed. Like other creatures of the island, the frogs have fallen prey to the cane toad. The full story of the frogs is still not known and is one of the many curiosities of the island.

The freshwater turtles of Fraser Island seem safe from natural predators but their numbers in some of the lakes have dwindled because visitors, captivated by their docile, engaging ways, have carried them off as pets. Lake Coomboo, in the centre of the island, is off the beaten track and in its tea-coloured waters the turtles thrive. There and in some of the other lakes and streams they are the hunters, not the hunted, creatures making the most of every available source of food.

There are three kinds of freshwater turtle on Fraser Island, all found elsewhere in Australia. They may have washed down to the sea in mainland streams in times of flood and floated across Great Sandy Strait on rafts of driftwood, then made their way inland from the west coast up to the streams and overland through the swamps to the dune

lakes. Perhaps the first colonisers waded across thousands of years ago when the sea level was much lower than the present and much of the strait was above water. Their long isolation from their mainland relatives and their food habits have produced characteristics that set them apart and the island's turtles may, in fact, have evolved to become a new species.

The most common turtle is Krefft's Tortoise which is also found along the Queensland coast east of the Great Dividing Range. The broad-shell turtle, Australia's largest long-necked turtle, on the island

Opposite: Early morning mist disperses in the sun over Lake Coomboo to reveal gnarled melaleucas among the reeds.

Left: High in the dunes Basin Lake hugs its secrets.

Below: Studies of the lifecycles of Fraser Island's freshwater turtles are helping unravel some of the mysteries of the great sand island.

nests in winter to avoid the summer 'wet' unlike others in temperate climates which nest in spring and summer. The common snake-necked turtle is an aggressive creature occurring in southern states as well as coastal Queensland to Cape York. Krefft's Tortoise shuns fast flowing streams, preferring the shoreline zones of the dune lakes where it finds most of its food.

On Fraser Island the Krefft's Tortoises are much smaller than their mainland counterparts and they lay fewer and smaller eggs. Young turtles are carnivorous, relying mostly on insects of the lake shores, and becoming less selective as they grow when their diets broaden to fuel their increasing energy needs. Scientists conclude that the island's turtles have only been able to survive and reproduce because they have adapted to draw on a wide variety of foods and because they have few predators and competitors in the lakes.

A series of studies concentrating on the nature of the lakes has provided a picture of the island's past, each discovery a piece of the jigsaw pointing the way towards understanding and properly managing Fraser Island. Hidden Lake, a small lake but the second deepest on the island, was chosen for the studies. Appropriately named, Hidden Lake nestles in a thickly wooded valley and twisted stems of paperbark trees encircle its shores.

In the middle of the lake floats a pontoon, a piece of space age equipment incongruous and at odds with the ageless atmosphere of the landscape. A few dabchicks swim past, unaware that the secrets of their enclosed world are being tapped by machines utilising one of mankind's most modern devices, nuclear weaponry. The lake experiments relate to radioactive fallout from nuclear weapons tested in Australia during the 1950s. In comparable mainland lakes such fallout filters down through the sediment, clearing the water of contamination. But this is not the case on Fraser Island. The amount of radio-activity is negligible and harmless, but its retention is a warning, an indication that the island's lakes have no way of ridding themselves from human litter, whether it comes from fallout, from mining or from just picknicking at the lakeside.

The chemical and physical studies look at accumulated sediments to give information about the way the waters respond to rainfall, overflow and evaporation and how the layers of different temperatures in the waters help preserve the organic sludge lying on the bottom. The deposits date back at least 10 000 years and indicate the changes that have taken place in that time. As part of the total environment, the lakes and their catchment areas have provided a means of studying the entire ecology of Fraser Island and predicting how possible changes may affect its future, with a view towards developing policies to conserve the unique island for future generations.

ACKNOWLEDGMENTS

Australian Defence Forces Academy; Australian National University; Australian Department of Defence; Australian Museum; Beach Protection Authority of Queensland; Brisbane College of Advanced Education Kelvin Grove Campus; Cameron McNamara and Partners Environmental Group, Brisbane; Canberra College of Advanced Education; Commonwealth Scientific and Industrial Research Organisation; CSIRO Division of Soils, Brisbane; Fraser Island Defenders Organisation; Griffith University; James Cook University; Mantis Wildlife Films; Glen Carruthers; Jim Frazier; Monash University; Queensland Department of Forestry; Queensland Institute of Technology; Queensland Museum; Queensland National Parks and Wildlife Service; Queensland Naturalists' Club; University of Melbourne; University of Queensland; University of Sydney.

Photographs used to illustrate this book were taken by members of Mantis Wildlife Films, Densey Clyne, Glen Carruthers and Jim Frazier.

Edited by Nina Riemer
Designed by Leigh Nankervis
Maps and diagrams by Michael Gorman

Published by ABC Enterprises for the
Australian Broadcasting Corporation
Box 9994 GPO Sydney NSW 2001
145 Elizabeth Street Sydney NSW

National Library of Australia
Cataloguing-in-Publication entry
Baverstock, Felicity
    Fraser Island, sands of time.
    ISBN 0 642 52992 2.
    1. Fraser Island (Qld.) – Description and
    travel. 2. Natural history – Queensland –
    Fraser Island. 3. Ecology – Queensland –
    Fraser Island. I. Clyne, Densey,
    1926- II. Australian Broadcasting
    Corporation. III. Title. IV. Title: Fraser
    Island, sands of time (Television
    program).
508.943'2

Set in 11/15pt Basilia Haas by BudgetSet,
Sydney
Printed and bound in Australia at The
Griffin Press, Adelaide
0109819 – 7.5M – 1995